From the maelstrom of a sundered world, the Eight Realms were born. The formless and the divine exploded into life. Strange, new worlds appeared in the firmament, each one gilded with spirits, gods and men. Noblest of the gods was Sigmar. For years beyond reckoning he illuminated the realms, wreathed in light and majesty as he carved out his reign. His strength was the power of thunder. His wisdom was infinite. Mortal and immortal alike kneeled before his lofty throne. Great empires rose and, for a while, treachery was banished. Sigmar claimed the land and sky as his own and ruled over a glorious age of myth.

But cruelty is tenacious. As had been foreseen, the great alliance of gods and men tore itself apart. Myth and legend crumbled into Chaos. Darkness flooded the realms. Torture, slavery and fear replaced the glory that came before. Sigmar turned his back on the mortal kingdoms, disgusted by their fate. He fixed his gaze instead on the remains of the world he had lost long ago, brooding over its charred core, searching endlessly for a sign of hope. And then, in the dark heat of his rage, he caught a glimpse of something magnificent. He pictured a weapon born of the heavens. A beacon powerful enough to pierce the endless night. An army hewn from everything he had lost. Sigmar set his artisans to work and for long ages they toiled, striving to harness the power of the stars. As Sigmar's great work neared completion, he turned back to the realms and saw that the dominion of Chaos was almost complete. The hour for vengeance had come. Finally, with lightning blazing across his brow, he stepped forth to unleash his creation.

The Age of Sigmar had begun.

CONTENTS

DESIGNED BY GAMES WORKSHOP IN NOTTINGHAM

Games Workshop Ltd., Willow Road, Lenton, Nottingham, NG7 2WS, United Kingdom

Printed by Leo Paper, in China.

games-workshop.com

THE IRONJAWZ

A booming roar rolls out across the Mortal Realms. Like an avalanche of hardened muscle and jagged-edged metal, the Ironjawz rampage through their foes. They are the biggest and meanest of the orruks, and under their massive choppas, empires and kingdoms are smashed to rubble.

Ironjawz are hulking brutes, always eager for a good scrap. As the largest members of a race infamous for their ferocity, they live only for war. Nothing is so pleasing to the ear of an Ironjaw as the sound of battle, of blades on armour and the screams of the dying. Taller and far broader than a man, they loom over their opponents, their battle-scarred hides encased in beaten iron armour. Fighting is everything to an Ironjaw orruk, for their small, brutish minds have room only for thoughts of wanton violence.

Under the vicious leadership of their bosses, mobs of Ironjawz stampede to battle. As they charge into the wild chaos of combat with weapons held high, the air vibrates to their long, deafening war cry of Waaagh!. Might makes right among the orruks, and none are as mighty as the Ironjawz. Over centuries of war, the races of the Mortal Realms have learned well to fear the coming of the Ironjaw warclans. The lost Empire of Shardlun, the wasteland where the Six Hundred Kingdoms once stood and the sunken Spires of Vys are all legacies of the Ironjawz. A green tide of ferocity, Ironjaw hordes rampage across the Mortal Realms in their countless millions, looking for armies to fight and cities to tear down, until all corners of the realms echo with their fury.

The Ironjawz are only just beginning their great war. It was during the Age of Chaos that they rose to power, thriving on the constant battle. Like the slowly growing rumble of a predator's growl, the Ironjaw warclans grew and expanded, until their mobs covered the lands. They fought against the beasts of the realms, human enclaves, other orruks, the armies of Chaos, and any others that crossed their path. For every battle they won, they grew in size and strength, and for every battle lost, they came back and fought all the harder. Soon, other orruks started to follow the Ironjawz about, reckoning that wherever there were Ironjawz there would always be a good rumble.

Gordrakk, the Fist of Gork, leads the Ironjawz on their Great Waaagh!.

Now a new age of war has begun, heralded by the crash of Sigmar's Storm, and the Ironjawz can smell violence in the air. The orruks' great two-headed god, Gorkamorka, has sensed it too. Eager for the coming carnage, he has sent a champion to lead the Ironjawz and their clans. Gordrakk, the Fist of Gork, is uniting the orruks under his pitiless gaze. For the first time in an age, the orruks are gathering in massive numbers for a Great Waaagh!. It will be an army so vast it will drown the realms in teeming greenskin armies until all that remains is smouldering ruins and shattered land.

In the vanguard of the Great Waaagh! will be the Ironjawz, earning their place among the clans by cracking skulls and smashing faces. At their head ride hulking Megabosses atop massive Maw-krusha mounts, surrounded by huge mobs of massive, ironclad Brutes. Charging past the Brutes, bellowing Gore-grunta cavalry barrel into the enemy, their eyes wild with battle lust. In their wake, crazed orruk shamans spew forth sorcerous energy, and rowdy Warchanters thump out a rhythm of destruction like the beat of mighty war drums heard in the distance. The races of the realms are starting to realise that the Great Waaagh! is stirring, and that the rumbling they feel shaking the land is the Ironjawz coming their way.

During the long Age of Chaos, the servants of the Dark Gods tried many times to crush the orruk clans. However, no matter how many greenskins fell under the blades of Chaos, more rose up to take their place, more numerous and ferocious than before.

Countless years of blood marked the first Chaos campaigns to vanquish the orruks, when Archaon's chosen general – Darkorn the Devourer – was charged with the task of wiping out the greenskins. Places like Splitbone Pass, where the bodies of Chaos Warriors lie as fallen leaves upon the ground, and the Sundeth Caves, which still echo to the cries of a thousand dying daemons, are monuments to the strength of the orruks. It speaks much to the futility of that war of extermination that today the orruks thrive across the realms, while Darkorn's skull adorns the gates of the Varanspire.

Among the orruk clans to rise from these centuries of carnage were the Ironjawz. Such is the nature of orruks, and Ironjawz especially, that the harder their enemies try to kill them, the harder they fight. Battling against Chaos hordes, human empires and other orruk clans with increasing brutality, the Ironjawz have become the largest of their kind. For them, the Age of Chaos was a gift from Gorkamorka, a time of joyous, unending battle that hammered their warclans into the toughest orruks around.

THE TWO-HEADED GOD

Gorkamorka is the twin-headed orruk god, and the greatest of the idols worshipped by the greenskins. During the Age of Myth, he crashed across creation leaving mighty fist-prints in the land as he waged war on everything in his path, while hordes of orruks followed him on his rampage of destruction.

For as long as orruks have plagued civilisation, the booming laughter and thunderous footsteps of Gorkamorka have resounded across the Mortal Realms. Gorkamorka is not one god but two, having long ago torn himself apart after a particularly spectacular falling out with himself. These two halves are known as Gork and Mork. Both gods share many aspects of the other, Mork being brutally cunning, while Gork is more cunningly brutal in nature. Crude images are often found smeared on walls, ruins and caves depicting Gork (or maybe Mork) hammering enemies with his club or stomping them under his great unwashed feet. When enough orruks gather together the two gods merge once more into Gorkamorka, working as one. Ironjawz follow Gork and Mork equally, calling out to one or the other depending on which is most likely to help them beat their victims to death.

Before he ripped himself in two, Gorkamorka was the feral champion in Sigmar's pantheon of gods, often first to be loosed on the foe. To win the orruk god's respect, Sigmar had to best him in contests of strength that raged all across Ghur and Azyr. Orruks tell stories of this time, trying to outdo each other with tales of their god's many scraps and his rivalry with the Hammer God. One such story tells of when Sigmar and Gorkamorka had an eating contest, grabbing up great fistfuls of the realms and stuffing them into their mouths. Sigmar ate a fiery mountain, so Gorkamorka drank an ocean. Sigmar inhaled the sky, his throat flickering with lightning, but Gorkamorka bested him by devouring the vast Kingdom of Thrun, and its people live in his belly to this day. Another tale recounts how the gods arm-wrestled over the Vargorth Shardplains, the mighty contest shattering their glass peaks and creating two great lakes. A tale told in Ghur says Gorkamorka took up Sigmar's hammer and knocked him clear across all eight realms, and the gods laughed afterwards at the devastation it had wrought. Even now, Ironjawz respect Sigmar's strength and know that his boys are always good for a fight.

THE DRUMBEAT OF WAAAGH!

Warchanters are the rabble-rousers of the Ironjawz and the closest thing they have to priests. Touched by the greenskin god, they hear a constant thumping hammering away in their heads. Ironjawz believe this is the twin heartbeat of Gork and Mork, which the Warchanter then drums in an endless, brutal rhythm with anything they can get their hands on. The heartbeat of Gork is slow and steady, a mighty thumping like the footsteps of a great beast loping toward its prey, while the heartbeat of Mork is fast and wild, echoing the stampeding feet of countless orruks as they charge into battle. The beating rhythm of the Warchanters accompanies the Ironjaw mobs to war and fills their enemies with fear. Sometimes, when Warchanters gather in mobs, the beat in their heads will grow louder and more violent until the ground shakes with the combined sound of their stikks. At these times, the greenskins think Gork (or maybe Mork) is speaking directly to them, and the message is always the same: go out and smash more faces.

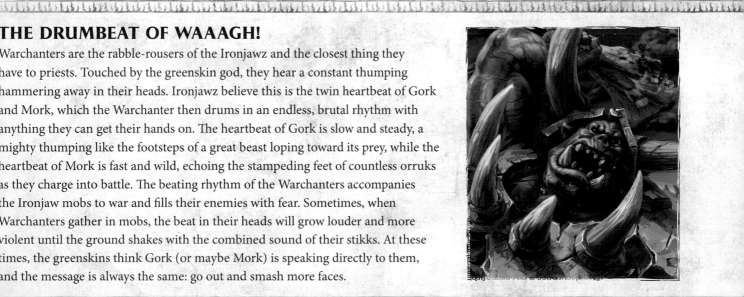

A BESTIAL REALM

The Ironjawz clan arose from the bestial wilds of Ghur and fought their way to dominate those lands. While they have since left trails of destruction across all the Mortal Realms, the Realm of Beasts still boasts the most Ironjawz and many of the greatest Megabosses come from its savage kingdoms.

Ghur is home to countless dangerous and violent lands where the strong survive and the weak become meat. This predatory wilderness suits the Ironjawz; endless wars against other orruks, slavering beasts and Chaos warriors mean their warclans have always had something to vent their savagery on. Just as an orruk boss imposes their dominance over their warclan, so too do the Ironjawz dominate the wildernesses of Ghur. Teetering effigies to Gorkamorka, splintered woodlands and mountains beaten into rubble are all signs left by the Ironjawz that they're in charge.

Once, the Realm of Beasts was filled with many noble empires ruled over by hunter kings and proud beast lords. Their domains were set atop snow-wreathed peaks or amid subterranean continents where mountains reached from above and below to form mazes of stone. Some stood on the backs of surging ocean monsters and others in the boughs of drifting sky-trees. The Ironjawz toppled one after another. If a skyborne keep flew the banners of free peoples or the eye-searing symbols of the minions of Chaos, it mattered not to the Ironjawz, only that the keep stood at all.

To stop the greenskins, their enemies constructed ever more elaborate defences – walls laced with killing spells, living moats that consumed all who crossed them, and cities with legs to carry them away from danger. But all failed before the simple, savage brutality of the Ironjawz.

As the Ironjaw armies laid waste to Ghur, they grew in size. Under the leadership of the mighty Megabosses, they formed their mobs into groups known as fists, and then even larger groups called brawls. Guided by these powerful greenskin warriors,

they spread out into the other Mortal Realms, following Gorkamorka's constant call to war into a thousand different lands.

Ironjawz do not build cities; they are a nomadic clan, wandering from one place to another looking for battle, and pausing only long enough to loot before moving on. As a warclan travels the realms, it will assert its dominance over everything it meets, either killing it or, in the case of other Ironjawz, adding them to their mob.

Orruks respect only strength, and other clans sometimes forget that the Ironjawz are in charge. Most clans are quickly knocked into line, though some, like the savage Bonesplittas, need constant reminding. By contrast, tribes of grots tend to steer clear of the Ironjawz, though they do occasionally

Gore-grunta Bosses know they are the best because they go the fastest.

join forces. Though they are not much use for fighting, some Ironjawz keep grots about for tasks such as sorting through scrap piles and dragging loot about, or to throw them into the grunta sty, which is always good for a laugh.

There can be no mistaking the handiwork of the Ironjawz. One of their most famous acts of vandalism was the defacement of the monolithic statue of Archaon which stood over the Manticore Realmgate that leads to the Allpoints. Three times have different Ironjaw warclans brought it down. The first time, the Everchosen's helm was recarved into the grinning face of Gork, so Archaon sent a legion to guard over its repair. The second time, the head was taken off entirely and replaced with a huge wooden grot head. Incensed, Archaon ordered the expansion of the Manticore Dreadhold. The third time, the Ironjawz brought down the walls and raised a crude idol to Gork over the fallen statue of Archaon. Now, a new Lord of Chaos commands the rebuilt Manticore Dreadhold, peering into the wastes as orruk drums rumble in the distance.

THE POWER OF THE WAAAGH!

When orruks gather, the ground shakes, violence boils over and the skies scream out in bestial rage. This is the power of the Waaagh! ready to unleash its brutal force upon the realms. The stronger an orruk army is, the mightier this energy becomes, and none are as strong as the Ironjawz.

Eyes wide with battle madness, muscles bunched into quivering cords and fists clenched tight around massive choppas, the Ironjawz are brutality wrapped in green flesh. When they gather, the atmosphere becomes thick with violence as killing energy fills the greenskins, their primeval roar building into a deafening boom as more voices join their rumbling war cry. Orruks do not think about the Waaagh! as others might think of magic, or the divine hand of gods or spirits. It is a force as primal as the orruks themselves, like the thundering of a warrior's heart in the heat of battle or the satisfying crunch of bone under a punch. Where mobs of orruks gather, there stirs a great green energy. Growing in power until it is as palpable as the scent of freshly spilt blood, it is vented upon victims with chopping blades and smashing boots. By the time it fades away, there is nothing left behind but beaten dust and the mangled remains of the greenskins' prey. All orruks know that their power grows stronger the harder they smash stuff and the louder they yell – two things Ironjawz excel at. Armies have been undone by the mere sight of a line of Ironjaw Brutes charging toward them, mouths opened wide revealing yellowed fangs and ropy strands of spit, as they unleash a gale of noisome breath and eardrum-bursting war cries.

Such a crusade of violence and destruction is known as a Waaagh!, a time when orruks rampage across the realms in numbers almost beyond count. During the long millennia of the Age of Myth and the Age of Chaos, there have been many of these bestial crusades, the fury of the greenskins cracking open continents, turning forest kingdoms into deserts and extinguishing whole races from existence. When this rampaging orruk energy flows strong, it can affect not only the greenskins but the very weft and weave of reality itself. Should enough orruks gather together, the land itself can rebel in violence. Beasts howl out war cries and orruk obscenities, trees rip their roots from the ground as they try to join the orruk charge, and rocks smash themselves to pebbles against each other. During the Shyish Splinterbone Wars, the power of Waaagh! Grungutz literally punched down the mile high wall of corpses surrounding the Gaunthavens,

A Waaagh! staff crackles with barely contained energy.

creating a cloud of bodies and debris that hung in the sky for a whole year. Similarly, the Waaagh! cry let loose by the Ironjawz during the Battle of Lone Peak boomed through every valley visible from the summit. So loud was the bellowing sound of the orruks, as they mercilessly pounded the warriors of the Gilded Legion into scrap metal, that it echoes on to this day.

If the Waaagh! is a howling gale that screams across the land, then orruk bosses are the canyons and passes that can focus its fury. Like the eye of a raging storm, Ironjaw Megabosses stand in the centre of seething mobs of orruks, directing their warclans. The greatest Megabosses, like Gordrakk, become blazing beacons of savage energy, drawing orruks from across the realms to fight for them. Combined with the Ironjawz' natural dominance over the other greenskin races, this can lead to vast and savage armies filled with countless howling orruk tribes, all intent on destruction.

There are legends of Megabosses whose Waaagh! energy was so strong it affected not only greenskins but other bestial races such as gargants, ogors and troggoths. It is said by the Weirdnob Shamans that such events are Gorkamorka's gift to the races of the realms, and a legacy of the first Great Waaagh! that never really ended.

WEIRDNOBS AND THE WAAAGH!

The power of the Waaagh! can take many forms, most of them violent, dangerous and unpredictable. In the Ironjaw warclans, it is the Weirdnob Shamans who unleash this wild green energy in some of its most spectacular effects. While a Megaboss is a focus for the power of the Waaagh!, amplifying it and drawing it toward themselves, Weirdnobs can release it with devastating, if erratic, results. Enemy wizards do well not to dismiss the cunning power of a Weirdnob Shaman as they stagger forward, eyes wide with mad intent. More than one sneering Tzeentchian Arcanite or sylvaneth Branchwraith has learned to their detriment that to enter into a magical duel with a Weirdnob is akin to sticking your face into a fire and hoping for the best.

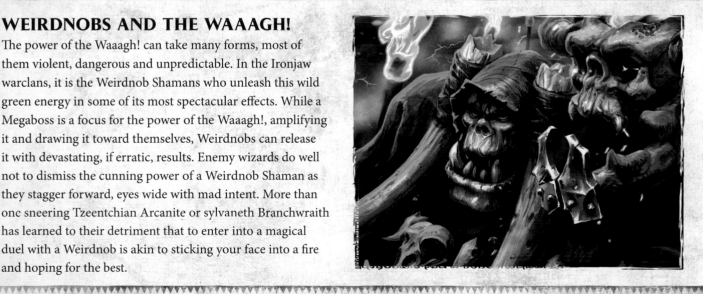

Under bruised skies, brutish roars clashed with howling prayers to the Dark Gods. Archaon's armies flowed like spilt blood across the Ugg Highlands of Ghur, a river of gore that crashed and parted around the Ironjaw warclans. With a thunderous boom the Stormcast Eternals arrived, riding twisting cords of lightning down from the sky. In a series of blindingly fast battles the Stormcasts tore apart the flanks of the Chaos horde, seeding the ground with their bodies at Mourn's Drift, the Weeping Maw and the Worldbone Peaks. Unimpressed, the Ironjaw Megabosses decided to crush these newcomers.

In a wave of violence, the orruks claimed the highlands back from Stormcast and Chaos worshipper alike. Sigmar's warriors were wrong-footed by the sudden attacks, and their strength was split between their enemies. At the Pigsnout Gate a Strike Chamber, wearied from protracted battles against Blood Warriors, made a defence against an Ironjaw charge that shook the walls of the canyon and raised great clouds of dust. Their disciplined shield wall was smashed into the dirt as a thousand Ironjawz surged out of the badlands to fall upon the Stormcasts. They eventually saw the wisdom in avoiding the Ironjawz where possible, leaving fortresses and enemies for them to crush in a faint reflection of the alliance once shared by Sigmar and Gorkamorka.

Ironjawz trampled the burning ground of the Cynder Peaks as Gordrakk led his warclan, the Fang-krushas, out of the wilderness looking for a fight. Back then, only a few clans knew about the Fist of Gork. The tales of how he cracked open the Kaverlos Doom Engine, felled the Everchosen's statue beneath the Manticore Gate, and ripped the head off Spittlefinger's Arachnarok with his bare hands were just spreading out across Ghur.

Gordrakk and the Fang-krushas gathered by the light of Grumbi's Furnace, the booming of their Warchanters calling forth Ironjawz from the burning wastes. By the time the Megaboss stood beneath the gates of the Dostev Magmahold, a hundred thousand orruks stood with him. In a battle that lasted for six seasons of flame, Gordrakk destroyed the Dostev Fyreslayer lodge, leaving naught but bones behind. As the lodge's forge-temple fell, a great green grin was seen up in the sky, and Gordrakk's name erupted from the lips of Weirdnob Shamans across the Mortal Realms. This was to be but the first of many omens that heralded the arrival of the Fist of Gork, and warclans bulled their way across the realms in search of this meanest of Megabosses. Other races, too, took note of the rise of Gordrakk. Archaon has sent scores of champions to claim the orruk's head, though so far none have returned – in one piece, that is.

THE BLESSED AND THE BRUTISH

Sigmar's grand alliance of the gods set Gorkamorka and the orruks at the side of the free peoples and their armies. Even so, the God-King kept a wary eye on the orruks, for the bestial warriors were often overzealous in their campaigns – setting allied kingdoms aflame and tearing down keeps to get to their enemies, all to the approving laughter of Gorkamorka.

THE FIRST WAAAGH!

TIRING OF SIGMAR'S QUEST FOR ORDER, GORKAMORKA BEGAN THE FIRST GREAT WAAAGH!. ORRUKS FLOCKED TO THE TWO-HEADED GOD, AND IN AN AVALANCHE OF GREEN FLESH THEY TORE A PATH OF RUIN ACROSS THE REALMS, ATTACKING THEIR FORMER ALLIES AND OLD ENEMIES WITHOUT DISTINCTION. WHEN GORKAMORKA CAME TO THE ABYSSAL WORLD'S END, HIS TWO SETS OF EYES GAZED FOR A MOMENT INTO THE FATHOMLESS DARK BEFORE HE SPAT OFF THE EDGE OF CREATION AND TURNED ABOUT TO DO IT ALL AGAIN.

THE AXE OF GORK AND MORK

Urrgrak Bonefist, the half-faced boss, became the first champion of Gorkamorka and was given the Worldchoppa, an axe said to have been made from iron ripped from Sigmar's throne. Millennia later, Gordrakk, the Fist of Gork, found the Worldchoppa and broke it into two axes to make it even more choppy.

CRUSHING JAWZ

When the first Ironjaw warclans emerged, they set about crushing all other orruks. Many bosses tried to challenge the dominance of the Ironjawz, and the realms shuddered to the violence unleashed. In the end, most clans either joined the Ironjawz or ended up as trophies on their armour.

FEAST OF THE GORE-GRUNTAS

The massive Ironsnout Warclan and its many Gorefists rode through every mountainous domain and kingdom of the Beastwold, feasting on everything in their path. Towns, forests and entire races were devoured by the gruntas. Their trail of ruin became known as the Goreroad and it is still in use to this day.

IN THE IRON SHADOW

Impressed by the strength of the Ironjawz, countless warclans gathered, hopeful to join them in their war against Chaos. The meanest of these formed Ardboy mobs, and marched into battle beside the massed armoured ranks of the Ironjaw Brawls.

THE BEAST KEEPS

ARCHAON'S LEGIONS SCOURED GHUR, HIS ARMIES TOPPLING EMPIRES AND SETTING LANDS AFLAME. ARCHAON'S REALM LORDS RAISED SKULL-BOUND KEEPS ACROSS THE LAND TO FETTER ITS INHABITANTS, BUT THE LORDS HAD NOT COUNTED ON THE IRONJAWZ. THE KEEPS WERE SWIFTLY OVERRUN OR PLACED UNDER CONSTANT SIEGE, AND THE BRUTES AND BOSSES OF MANY IRONJAW WARCLANS BECAME ADEPT AT SMASHING APART WHATEVER DEFENCE CHAOS COULD MUSTER.

THE BRUTAL LEGION

During the Age of Chaos, the impossibly vast Forest of Claws belonged to the Facesmasha Warclan and its Brutefists. When the warriors of the Darkflesh Warhorde marched into the wood to destroy the orruks, its regiments were consumed in a storm of violence. For days, screams, the clash of steel and bestial war cries drifted on the wind. Of the legions of Darkflesh warriors, none returned, though soon, Facesmasha Brutes were seen wearing the beaten remains of Chaos armour.

THE TWO-HEADED BOSS

Weirdfists and Ironfists formed the two brutal arms of the Cracktoof Warclan. Throughout the Sundercave War, Megaboss Urrgok and Weirdnob Shaman Zzadak fought for control of the clan, even as they battled Tzeentch Arcanites. Only when a chance Tzeentchian spell cast Zzadak's mind into Urrgok's body did the Cracktoof Warclan finally unite under the 'two-headed' boss Zzagok, much to the woe of the Arcanites.

THE TRAIL OF GORK

AS THE IRONJAWZ GREW IN POWER ACROSS THE REALMS, CUNNING BOSSES FIGURED OUT THE IMPORTANCE OF REALMGATES WHEN IT CAME TO FINDING A GOOD SCRAP. CRUDE ORRUK GLYPHS OF GORK (OR MAYBE MORK) BEGAN TO APPEAR ON GATEWAYS ACROSS THE MORTAL REALMS. THEIR PRESENCE WAS AN INVITATION AND A CHALLENGE TO ANY IRONJAWZ WHO CAME ACROSS THEM, AND A WARNING TO ALL OTHERS.

IRON IS IRON

Ironjaw Brutes of the Dethfist Warclan invaded the Daemon Pits of Gorrmurg, rampaging among its Soul Grinder pens. Tearing iron from the war machines, the orruks hammered the daemon metal into armour. Even though the living iron continually tried to crush them, the Brutes took great pride in their new armour, as it just proved how 'super killy' they must be.

THE DEAD ONES

WAAAGH! DRAKGRUZ PLOUGHED INTO THE NIGHTLANDS OF SHYISH FOLLOWING THEIR BLOODY-MINDED MEGABOSS UPON HIS ONE-EYED MAW-KRUSHA. DISCOVERING VAST EMPIRES OF DEATHRATTLERS THAT THEY COULD DESTROY AGAIN AND AGAIN, THE IRONJAWZ EMBARKED ON A WHIRLWIND OF DESTRUCTION SO INTENSE IT CREATED A DUSTSTORM OF BONE SHARDS. DRAKGRUZ' WARCLANS BECAME AS PALE SPECTRES, COVERED IN WHITE BONE DUST, SAVE THE SAVAGE DARKNESS IN THEIR EYES.

A KRUSHING DEFEAT

Atop his great Maw-krusha, Thung, Daggrog led his warclan and a dozen other beast-mounted Megabosses to smash the Grond Magmagates, trampling its Fyreslayer defenders into the dirt and ending the Ironpeak War.

BLOOD FOR GORK

While in the Ashlands, the Ironeye Warclan discovered vast mounds of skulls and proceeded to smash them down. Soon, violent, red-clad warriors arrived, and the orruks realised that wrecking such monuments was a good way to get the Bloodbound riled up.

A TOO-CUNNIN' PLAN

Skaven warlock Skeez Volt-tail hatched a plan to manipulate the Dakhammaz warclan into destroying his Fyreslayer foes. Expecting the two forces to annihilate each other, Skeez waited until the sounds of battle faded before making his entrance. To his horror, he found the Ironjawz still standing, only too happy for a new fight.

FULL METAL WAR-STY

When thousands of Gore-gruntas attacked the Chaos citadels of Anvrok in Chamon, their steeds' hides and tusks transformed to living iron under the light of the Alchemist's Moon, creating a huge metallic war-sty.

DA LAST BOSS

FIVE WARCLANS MET AMID THE CARNAGE OF THE BLOOD TIMES. FOR DAYS, THEY SMASHED EACH OTHER TO BITS. WEIRDNOBS DUELLED WHILE BRUTES CLASHED TO THE FRENZIED BEAT OF HUNDREDS OF WARCHANTERS, BUT NONE COULD BEST THE OTHERS. THEIR LEADERS WERE SCARRED AND SPENT FROM THEIR EXERTIONS WHEN GORDRAKK FOUND THEM. LAUGHING AT THEIR STRUGGLES, HE TOOK THE WARCLANS FOR HIS OWN AND MADE THEIR FIVE MEGABOSSES INTO HIS PERSONAL BODYGUARD, KNOWN AS THE MEGAFIST.

A WEIRD GATHERING

A dozen Weirdnobs were inexplicably drawn to the Groaning Mountain of Ghur. As the sylvaneth hosts held back the shamans' brawl on the slopes of the living peak, the Weirdnobs began to spasm, until a vast green fist punched the mountain into the sea.

ACTS OF RANDOM VIOLENCE

Across the realms, orruks complicated the plans of the far-seeing seraphon, for the savage whims of the greenskins were almost impossible to predict. Cunning Ironjaw bosses figured out that the seraphon always seemed to be fighting the forces of the Dark Gods, and some went so far as to paint their boys up like Chaos warriors to fool the seraphon into attacking them.

KINGDOMS OF SCRAP

To his annoyance, Megaboss Rutkag reduced the Cogoth Copperlands to rubble and thereby ran out of foes to fight. Never ones to let good scrap go to waste and impatient for a good fight, Rutkag's Ironjaw warclan divided into a dozen fragments, each one building teetering ruin-forts from the rubble, and they waged a long yet satisfying war against each other.

DRUMS OF WAAAGH!

The Warchanter Bonzog wandered the realms rousing Ironjawz and countless other orruks to war. Following the drumming beat in his head, Bonzog sought out places where he could hammer out his message at a deafening volume. The Hollow Peaks of Garm, the Gilded Worldbell and the Ringing Crystal Forests of Ghyran all echoed to the thunder of his stikks. As he travelled, other Warchanters joined Bonzog, each orruk eager to share the beat of war.

BIG WAAAGH!

As the Age of Sigmar dawned, the shadow of Gordrakk stretched across the realms like a great raised fist. Chaos castellans kept a wary eye on the horizon, and in the depths of their holds, the fyreslayers felt the ground shaking, while in the wilds of Ghyran the sylvaneth sensed that a great predator drew near. Even the Stormcast Eternals could feel a growing rumbling fit to rival the Storm of Sigmar in all its fury.

DA BOSS KEEP

High in the Shardlung Peaks, Megaboss Kagrak captured the Crookblade Chaos Dreadhold from the Warhaunters tribe. Such was the determination of the Warhaunter lords and their armies to reclaim the fortress, Kagrak decided to keep the castle. Soon its skull-lined walls and towers were covered in orruk glyphs.

LIGHTNING IRON

Though countless Ironjawz tried to loot sigmarite from the Stormcasts, the metal always vanished before it could be claimed. Instead, to make it clear that they were just as impressive as Sigmar's boys, some clans settled for painting their iron to match the Stormcasts' shining plate.

FORCES OF THE IRONJAWZ

IRONCLAD ARMIES

Ironjaw armies are made up of rowdy mobs of thuggish warriors who care naught for fancy banners or ordered ranks. As they bull their way into battle, the largest take the lead, trampling any who get between them and their enemies. For the Ironjawz, there's only one rule: the big ones make the rules.

The organisation of Ironjaw warclans is as chaotic and brutal as the Ironjaw orruks themselves. Their greenskin armies are built from huge unruly mobs, gathered into fists and then smashed together by Megabosses into brawls. Ironjawz, like most orruks, don't bother with pointless things like poetry, personal hygiene or numbers above five. The basic building block of all their formations is the mob, which is led by a boss, and can be any size. Five orruks is a mob, but so is five hundred. While orruks are not great at counting how many boys are in a mob, those on foot and those on gruntas tend to stick together. This is more a natural by-product of the fastest Ironjawz getting to the fight first than it is about 'taktiks'.

Things get more 'precise' when it comes to organising multiple mobs. These are gathered into fives, one for each finger a Megaboss can count on. These mob gatherings are known as fists, and just like the bunched fingers of an orruk, they are great for smashing stuff. In fact, this is often how a Megaboss will form a fist, showing a mob boss an open hand before closing the fingers and thumping them, much to the amusement of all involved. It is a brutally effective method of organisation and one that has worked for the Ironjawz for as long as any of them can remember. Not all Megabosses are created equal, however, and some have trouble getting even to five, especially if they have lost fingers or, worse, whole hands. Others are rare

and talented generals, at least by orruk standards, and have discovered that if they hold both their hands next to each other, they can get to ten. Rumours tell of mysterious barefoot orruks that can count even higher, but most Ironjawz don't believe such fantastical tales.

Sometimes, a fist will be led by a Warchanter or Weirdnob Shaman instead of a Megaboss. Warchanters lead huge processions of rumbling, chanting orruks, Ironjawz and Ardboys massing behind them. Weirdnobs are the bane of sorcerers and magical hosts alike, and the Waaagh! energies created by a Weirdfist are released as crackling bolts of power at any unsuspecting army foolish enough to be in their path.

IRONJAW LEADERSHIP

Armies of Ironjawz seem to respond in an almost instinctual way to the presence of foes. To their enemies, the battlefield behaviour of the orruks can appear simple and blunt, but beneath the roiling greenskin ranks is a unity of purpose few armies possess. At the centre of the Ironjaw leadership are hard-headed bosses keeping the boys in line. Much of orruk language involves delivering backhanded blows and well-timed headbutts. A Megaboss can explain their entire strategy to a boss by giving them a sharp clip around the ear, the underling knowing at once what is expected of them. This is the foundation of all orruk battle plans; the biggest ones take charge over anyone they can smack about and take orders from anyone who can knock them down. Orruks accept this as a fundamental law, and often have trouble understanding why other races follow leaders just because they know magic stuff, own a flashy fort or wear a big hat – though some warclans have, in the past, tried to make the big hat system of leadership work, albeit with little success.

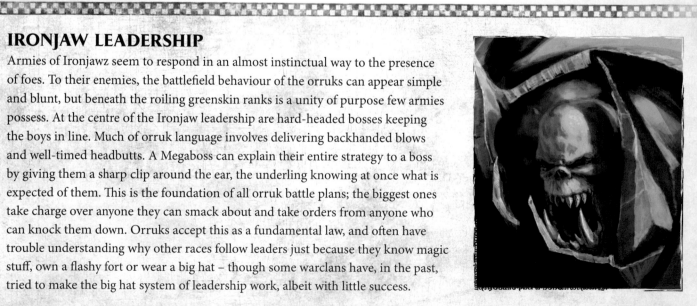

When a group of fists are fighting together, they are collectively known as a brawl. Typically, a brawl will be five fists bashed together under the leadership of a single Megaboss. Unlike the more rigid military structures of other races, a brawl is not a permanent thing, even though it might fight together under a single, iron-fisted Megaboss for years or decades of unadulterated violence.

Brawls are not created in the marshalling yards of keeps or cities, but are usually formed in the heat of battle. No orruk worth their teeth would follow someone they didn't know was good in a scrap, so Ironjawz join brawls more by proximity than intent. A Megaboss will stand on the back of their Maw-krusha, or perhaps scale a mound of broken enemy bodies, and make it clear with a wave of their choppa that all the fists they can see are now part of their brawl. Ironjawz take this kind of leadership in their stride, and if the boss orruk on the Maw-krusha says go smash up that keep, who are they to argue?

Brawls are used as weapons by any Megaboss powerful enough to keep one together, and their agendas are usually quite simple. If a fortress is barring the path, or a powerful monster or famous general makes their presence known nearby, this is all the excuse needed for a brawl to form. Brawls made up of Brutefists are used as battering rams against any defence hoping to stand against the Ironjawz. Cloud-piercing battlements and spike-riddled moats are simply seen as invitations to the Ironjawz, who are always eager to rip down walls or pile over obstacles to get to a good fight. Brawls of Gore-gruntas tend to overwhelm their prey with sudden speed and terrifying strength, although the gruntas might sometimes stop to feed upon fallen enemies despite the roaring of their riders.

25

WARCLANS

Ironjaw warclans can be found in almost every corner of the Mortal Realms, their bellowed war cries echoing from the shadowy depths of Shyish to the gleaming kingdoms of Chamon. Led by bloody-minded Megabosses, warclans are shaped both by their brutal leaders and the lands they savage.

Ironjaw warclans can come in almost any size, ranging from a single Megaboss, Warchanter or Weirdnob Shaman followed by a motley army of boys, all the way up to continent-spanning Ironjaw 'empires' made up of scores of Megabosses and many brawls, all under the iron rule of a single massive Megaboss. It is a well-known fact that the more an Ironjaw warclan fights, the bigger it gets; additional Ironjawz are summoned by the sound of battle, while an ascendant Megaboss grows physically larger as the Waaagh! intensifies around them. It is a process that continues to rampage out of control until either the Ironjawz run out of enemies and turn on each other, or their leader is slain and usurped by a bigger, stronger Megaboss.

Most warclans' names are bestowed by the Megaboss that battered them together, and are usually something descriptive intended to impress and intimidate other clans and enemies. The Bloodgrins, for instance, wipe their mouths in the blood of those they've defeated and leave bloody handprints on their armour, faces and gruntas. Dethtoofs paint their teeth black, or replace them with bits of shiny black rock, the fangs of monsters, or razor-sharp metal fragments. Ironjawz of the Stoneskulls Warclan paint their iron bone-white like the skeletons of the dead they leave behind.

Many warclans take their name from the place where they were formed. These include the dun-armoured Ironclawz from the Forest of Claws, the black-armoured Asheater Boyz of the Soot Peaks or the Brutes of the Skybasha Warclan who plunder the skyways in their airborne scrap-hulks.

A powerful boss might also lend their own name to a warclan, as in the case of Doggrok's Choppas, Zedek's Weirdladz or the Hooktoof Scrappas. Gordrakk's infamy is a prime example of this, and the number of warclans bearing his name or moniker, the Fist of Gork, grows with each passing day.

Gore-choppas are devastating weapons in the hands of an orruk Brute.

Some warclans keep the name of a dead Megaboss, often along with their remains, as a sort of trophy. These Ironjawz like to claim that this means they are never defeated, as was the case with the Grok Skullz Warclan, who carried the skull of Megaboss Grok with them for centuries so he could oversee the final destruction of the clan's enemies.

Gordrakk's original warclan, the Fang-krushas, have followed a slightly unusual path, and are now typically led by a Megaboss from his Megafist, alongside the many other warclans who have joined in his ever-growing Waaagh!. They have kept their name, however, and are more than a little smug and boastful about their association with the Fist of Gork, whether the other warclans believe them or not.

Regardless of their name, a warclan's sole reason for existing is to fight, and fight some more. Raising idols, good looting and destructive vandalism are all secondary to the act of expending their strength as violently and as often as they can. In this sense, warclans are purely catastrophic forces, moving across the land destroying anyone or anything with the audacity to be in the way. For every great warclan that walks the realms, there is a trail of broken empires and shattered lands left behind.

IRONJAW WARCLAN

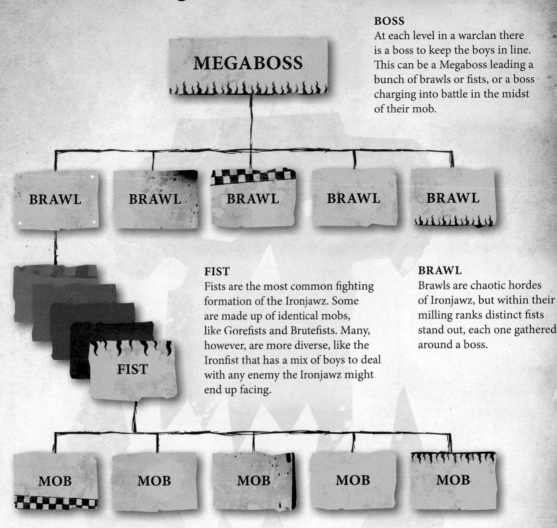

MEGABOSS

BRAWL BRAWL BRAWL BRAWL BRAWL

FIST

MOB MOB MOB MOB MOB

BOSS
At each level in a warclan there is a boss to keep the boys in line. This can be a Megaboss leading a bunch of brawls or fists, or a boss charging into battle in the midst of their mob.

FIST
Fists are the most common fighting formation of the Ironjawz. Some are made up of identical mobs, like Gorefists and Brutefists. Many, however, are more diverse, like the Ironfist that has a mix of boys to deal with any enemy the Ironjawz might end up facing.

BRAWL
Brawls are chaotic hordes of Ironjawz, but within their milling ranks distinct fists stand out, each one gathered around a boss.

MOB
A mob is a catch-all name for a group of Ironjawz, and can be anything from a few orruks to a few hundred in number. To make beating things up easier, and to help the Megaboss keep track of all the killing, mobs tend to contain Ironjawz armed with the same weapons.

SHAMANS

WARCHANTERS

Weirdnob Shamans sometimes boss about mobs, fists and brawls, but they will also follow a powerful Megaboss, charging up off all of the boss' Waaagh! energy.

Warchanters can lead mobs, fists and even brawls. Most of the time, though, they run about like madboys, getting everyone riled up with their endless drumming.

IRONJAW BRAWL

Like the fingers of a fist curling together to beat the life out of someone, the orruks of an Ironjaw brawl come together to make war. From its massive Maw-krushas and Megabosses down to its mobs of brawny Brutes and regimented Ardboys, it is a clanking, bellowing tide of ill-tempered green flesh.

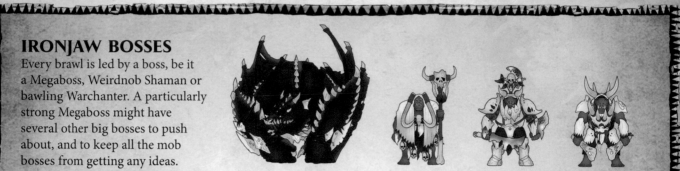

IRONJAW BOSSES

Every brawl is led by a boss, be it a Megaboss, Weirdnob Shaman or bawling Warchanter. A particularly strong Megaboss might have several other big bosses to push about, and to keep all the mob bosses from getting any ideas.

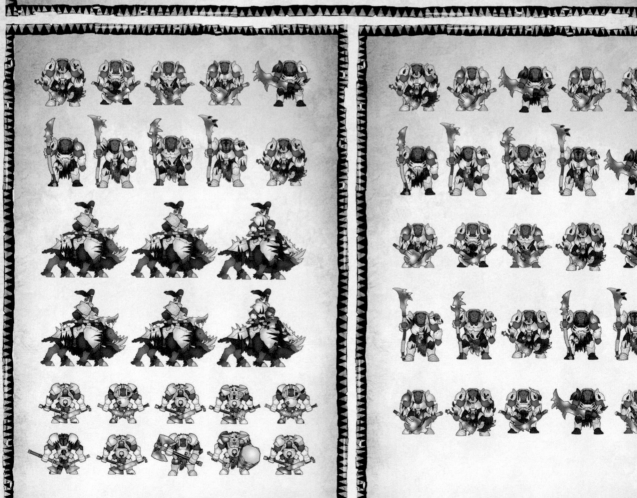

IRONFIST

Ironfists are versatile formations with a mix of Brutes, Gore-gruntas and Ardboys – Brutes for smashing, Gore-gruntas for charging, and Ardboys for all the other stuff.

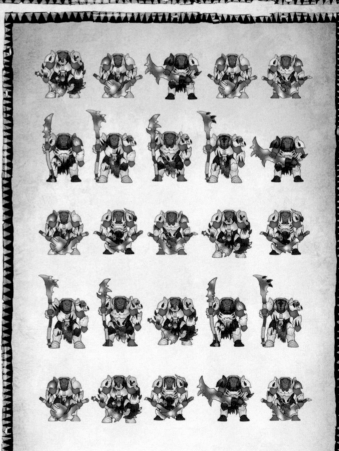

BRUTEFIST

Few things compare to the overwhelming force of a Brutefist, its Ironjawz beating, smashing and battering everything in their path.

GOREFIST

Gorefists are massed mobs of Gore-gruntas, all thundering across the battlefield as fast as they can to slam into the enemy. In battle they are often part of a Megaboss' 'taktiks', attacking flanks and other soft bits of the opposing army.

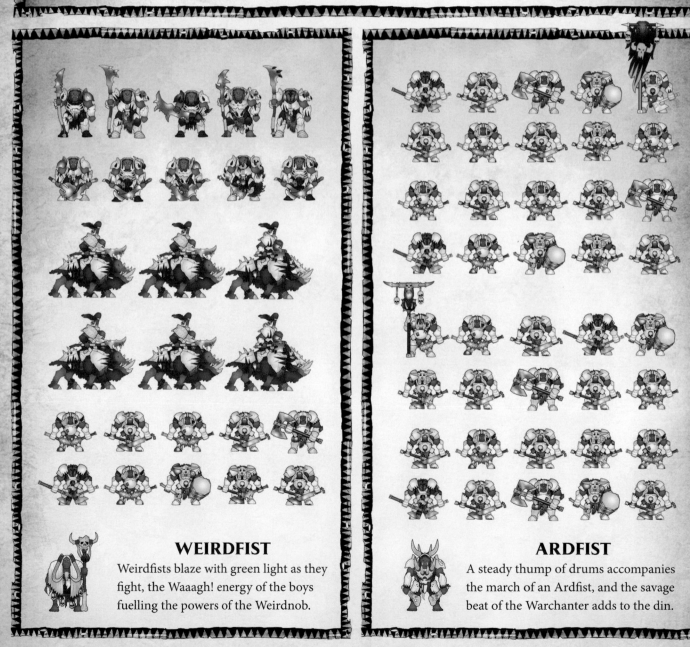

WEIRDFIST

Weirdfists blaze with green light as they fight, the Waaagh! energy of the boys fuelling the powers of the Weirdnob.

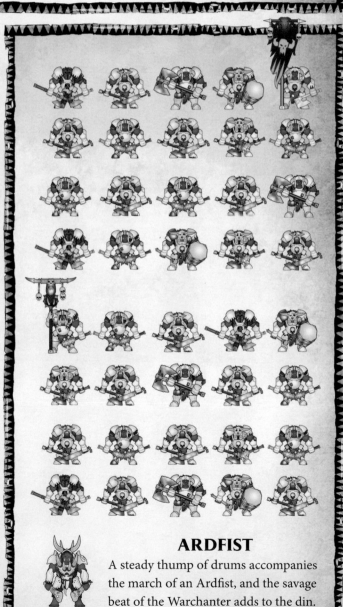

ARDFIST

A steady thump of drums accompanies the march of an Ardfist, and the savage beat of the Warchanter adds to the din.

DAKKBAD'S IRONSUNZ

The Ironsunz are one of the largest warclans to fight in Gordrakk's Waaagh!. Mobs wearing their flashy yellow armour can be seen in almost every realm, and the Ironsunz throw their weight around making sure everyone knows that they are the best.

Megaboss Dakkbad Grotkicker has risen to rule the Ironsunz over a trail of bashed-in skulls and broken bones. The previous Megaboss of the Ironsunz, Gutdrukk Fourfist, made the mistake of keeping Dakkbad around. Unfortunately for Gutdrukk, Dakkbad encouraged the Megaboss through a Realmgate to the heart of the Bloodspire Chaos Dreadhold, and then smashed up the gate so that – he claimed – none of the Chaos Warriors could get away. Everyone knows that Dakkbad is cunning, and some orruks even reckon he might have an eye on Gordrakk's position. If the Fist of Gork is concerned about this, he hasn't let on. If Dakkbad ever decides to have a go at usurping the Great Waaagh!, he had better make it count, because if he fails, the last thing he'll see is the edge of Gordrakk's axe.

SUNZ OF IRON

Ironsunz are notorious for throwing their weight around, lording their place in Gordrakk's Great Waaagh! over the other warclans and stomping about in their flashy yellow armour. They are, however, both cunning and good at giving out kickings, so most boys know better than to mess with them.

Megabosses strap the biggest trophies they can find onto their armour, to prove they are the biggest and meanest.

Even though they don't wear armour, Weirdnob Shamans wrap themselves in robes of their warclan's colours.

Warchanters often festoon their armour with horns and bones to make themselves even more fearsome.

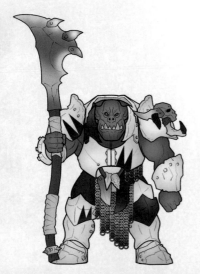

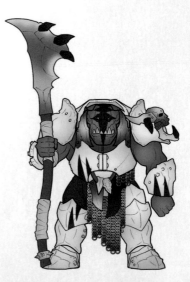

The red markings on the Ironsunz' armour represent teeth, flames or claws depending on which orruk is telling the story. All agree, though, that on the yellow Ironsunz plates, they look dead scary and especially killy.

Sometimes, Ironjawz will have mismatched bits of iron on their armour and weapons that they have not yet got around to painting in the warclan colours. They might deliberately leave it this way if they want to show off a shiny choppa or boss klaw.

Gruntas are covered in jagged bits of iron, some painted in the colours of the clan, others shiny, rusty or stained.

Grunta riders like to paint some of the red 'teef' on their mount's armour horizontally to make them go faster.

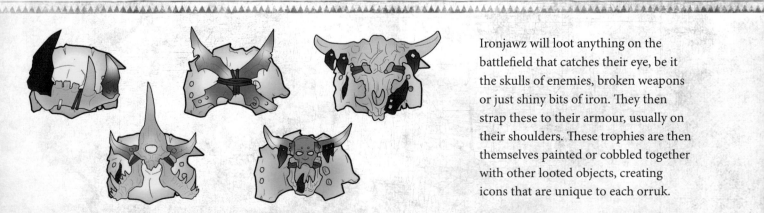

Ironjawz will loot anything on the battlefield that catches their eye, be it the skulls of enemies, broken weapons or just shiny bits of iron. They then strap these to their armour, usually on their shoulders. These trophies are then themselves painted or cobbled together with other looted objects, creating icons that are unique to each orruk.

Dakkbad Grotkicker carries with him the skull of the legendary Chaos Lord Felgraen Hexflayer, so no one will ever forget just how hard he is. Skullzcrakka, Dakkbad's Maw-krusha, wears armour painted in similar colours to his master, and his red and black scale colouration mean he was probably reared in the trackless wilderness somewhere deep within fiery Aqshy.

The brass plates on this Brute were likely scavenged from Khornate warriors, always a good source of iron.

Especially lucky Ironjawz get to carry Gore-choppas, which are left as raw iron to show how shiny they are.

Brutes often add extra 'teef' to their weapons using whatever iron they can find, giving them more bite.

Ardboys carry standards to identify themselves, like this one holding up the symbol of the Ironhorn mob.

The iron gob of Gork is a common icon of the Ardboys, and also makes for a pretty good weapon.

The Scrapskull mob bear the symbol of the iron skull, and they all go to battle wearing full face helms.

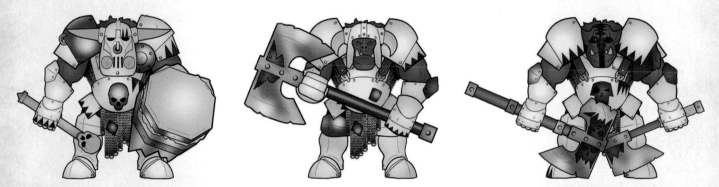

To maintain discipline, Ardboys have musicians with massive iron drums bound in the same metals as their armour. Also keeping order are hulking bosses, usually armed with the biggest weapons they can lay their hands on.

These Ardboys wear the yellow and red colours of the Ironsunz to show they are part of the warclan. However, just as they are not true Ironjawz, so too is their armour slightly different, neater and with more precise red teeth than that of the Brutes.

BLOODTOOFS WARCLAN

To find the best fights means finding the Fist of Gork. The Bloodtoofs know this, and so their hordes of crimson mobs fight across the Mortal Realms looking for the legendary Gordrakk. Megaboss Zogbak Realmrippa knows his warclan is the best, and so assumes that the Great Waaagh! must be waiting for him somewhere.

Always on the move, the Bloodtoofs hunt out Realmgates, looking for the one Gordrakk is on the other side of. Along the way, they aim to win as many fights as they can, and took time from their hunt to cut down the Singing Oak of Faeious, silencing its gentle song with their choppas and giving its guardians a good stomping to boot. In the Penumbral Vault, the Flesh-eater Court of Marrowthirst felt the Bloodtoofs' wrath when the Ironjawz smashed into the king's menagerie and turned his clutch of zombie dragons into a twitching idol to Gork (or Mork, depending on the angle). No territory or kingdom is safe from the Bloodtoof's violence, as Zogbak leads them through one Realmgate after another, seeking the biggest scrap.

THE BLOODTOOFS

Eager for battle, the Bloodtoofs Warclan paint their armour red, the colour of blood and war. Whether this is because they see red as the fightiest colour or so they can easily see where their boys are going – and thus find the best fights – is unclear, but there are few sights are fearsome as this tide of red iron.

Megaboss Zogbak gets the pick of the best bits of iron; these dark plates contrast with the rest of his armour.

Weirdnob Shaman Zzapdak has a good collection of wizard skulls that he often talks to about 'magic stuff'.

A Warchanter's stikks are his prized possessions, and more important than fancy things like choppas or boots.

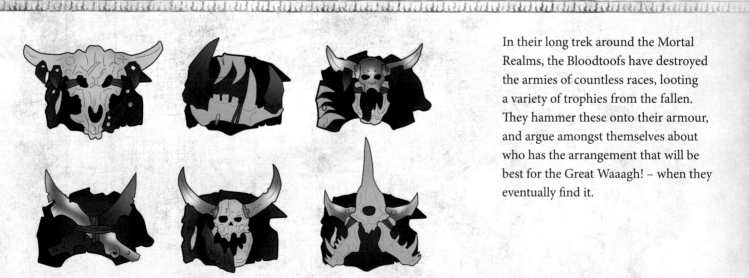

In their long trek around the Mortal Realms, the Bloodtoofs have destroyed the armies of countless races, looting a variety of trophies from the fallen. They hammer these onto their armour, and argue amongst themselves about who has the arrangement that will be best for the Great Waaagh! – when they eventually find it.

Bloodtoof Ironjawz paint yellow wavy teeth onto their armour, sometimes representing kill markings, with a single 'toof' representing a big monster. Bloodtoof Brute bosses always get the best trophies and have flashier bits of iron and bone.

Bloodtoof grunta riders paint teeth around the eye holes of their mounts, believing it makes them more aggressive.

Ironjaw Brutes cobble together their armour, adding or discarding bits as they seem useful or a hindrance.

Brute skull trophies sometimes have iron gobs added to them.

Over time, a good gore-choppa will have new bits of metal added to it.

Dark iron is thought to be the best, and is used by the hardest Ironjawz.

Megaboss Krugok Neckstomper has hammered brass teeth around his neck so he can headbutt and 'bite' at the same time. His Maw-krusha, Razok, has stone and steel skin from its battles in Chamon, causing its hide to shimmer dully as it moves.

Bloodtoof Ardboys often make metal skulls to hammer onto their armour rather than real skulls, which tend to break in battle. Their weapons, unlike those of true Ironjawz, don't include what they see as shoddy materials like wood or bone.

Ardboys' shoulder plates are made from layered iron, often from different sources, then painted in their warclan's colours. Like their creators, orruk designs are often loud and to the point.

The Flameskullz Ardboys fight with the Bloodtoofs under their burning skull icon, usually adorned with trophies from their most recent battles. Flameskull drummers use the skulls of their foes to beat out the march to war.

Grunta riders like to add pointy bits of iron to their armour and that of their mounts, and paint them so they stand out.

Bloodtoof Gore-gruntas often have beast-hair topknots dyed in bright colours so their enemies can see them coming.

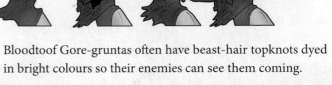

REALMS OF IRON

Just as Ironjawz change the lands they rampage through with violence, so too do the lands change them. Warclans often have their own unique appearances, depending on the iron they scavenge, the enemies they have crushed, or the environments they have fought in.

Asheater Boyz of the Ghyran Soot Peaks paint their armour with the incinerated remains of sylvaneth, just because they can. They also paint some of their iron red and white to look like blood and bone, showing off just how brutal they are.

Doggrok's Choppas are led by the Weirdnob Shaman Ka-rokk, who carries about Doggrok's skull on a stick. Ka-rokk says Doggrok told him to tell the boys to paint war-checks on their armour, and no one dares argue with Doggrok, alive or dead.

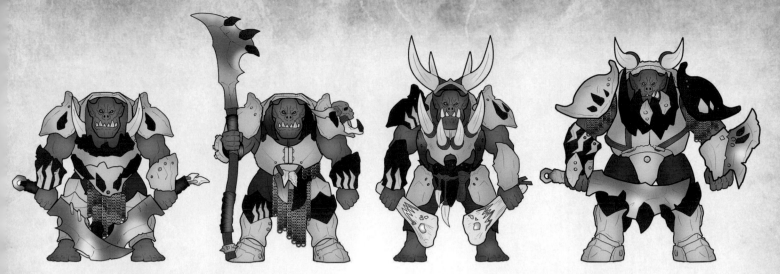

Stoneskulls paint their armour a distinctive bone white so their foes know who is clobbering them. The warclan also add crimson 'teef' and flame designs to go with all the normal mess of killing stuff that inevitably ends up on them.

Zedek's Weirdladz are led by the Weirdnob Shaman Zedek, who is well known for setting things on fire, mostly on purpose. The warclan's orange and black armour makes the few inevitable burning orruks less distracting as their mobs charge into battle.

The Skybasha Warclan make their armour from shiny sky-iron. However, they still want to look like they mean business so they paint red teeth onto their armour, and red on their best weapons – like their boss klaws – so no one thinks they have gone soft.

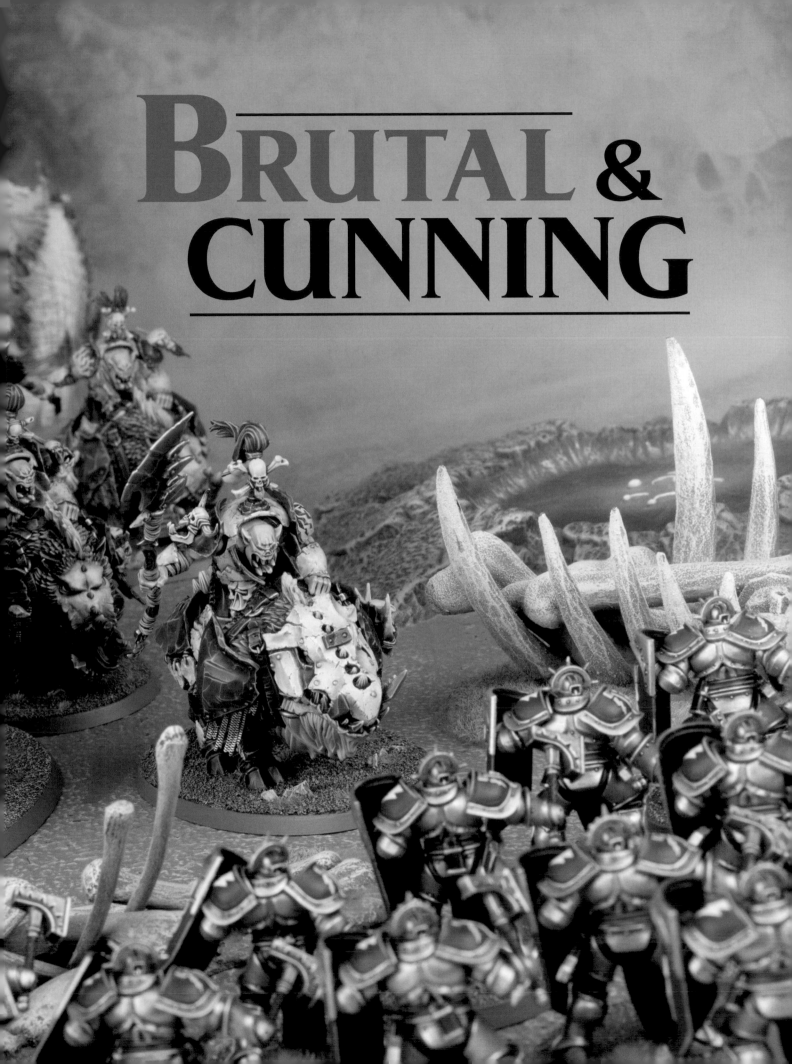

BRUTAL & CUNNING

GORDRAKK, THE FIST OF GORK

Amid the bellowing and bawling of the Ironjawz, a single mighty voice booms out above all the rest. This is Gordrakk, the Fist of Gork and undisputed boss of bosses. A hulking warlord of prodigious size, he is an unstoppable force of destruction and herald of the next Great Waaagh!.

Every orruk has heard of Gordrakk, the Fist of Gork. His name is the war cry upon the lips of a billion charging Ironjawz, the screams of dying men crushed under hobnailed orruk boots, and the thunderous chant of marching greenskins as they spill out across the realms. Chosen by Gorkamorka, Gordrakk will cover all the realms with the hordes of his Great Waaagh!.

During the Age of Chaos, the minions of the Dark Gods tried to enslave the Ironjawz of Ghur, building countless Dreadholds throughout the wild kingdoms. Taking exception to these edifices, Gork slammed his continent-sized fist into the Wildheart, a monolithic green storm of energy descending from the sky to pound the fortresses into the ground. When Gork's fist vanished, it left behind a smouldering fragment of knucklebone, and as the green fires seared away its surface, a hulking Megaboss was revealed. Whether or not this tale of his origins is true, Gordrakk has become known as the Fist of Gork and does nothing to dispute the story. Some even say that in Gordrakk's good eye, one can still see the bunched knuckles of Gork, a moment before the Megaboss smashes their face in.

Even by the standards of the Ironjawz, Gordrakk is a warrior of vicious cunning and bestial ferocity. The scars

Smasha and Kunnin' are Gordrakk's twin axes of destruction.

of his rampages can be seen across the Mortal Realms in desolate fields of broken bodies and mangled iron stretching out as far as the eye can see. His twin axes, Smasha and Kunnin', have claimed the heads of heroes and kings alike, one weapon blessed with brutal cunning by Mork, the other with the cunning brutality of Gork. These blades were once a single great axe known as the Worldchoppa, but Gordrakk broke it in two so he could do more killing.

As befits a Megaboss as mean as Gordrakk, he rides a ferocious mount to war. Covered in thick calloused scales, Bigteef is a humongous Mawkrusha with beady eyes and yellowed teeth. In battle, the beast wades through combats, pounding enemies to pulp, even as Gordrakk hacks open bodies

and crushes skulls with his twin axes. There are many tales told by wild-eyed Weirdnobs and babbling Warchanters as to how a belligerent beast like Bigteef came to submit to the yoke of Gordrakk. Some tell of how the Mawkrusha was so vicious that anything he looked at died of fright, their hearts bursting before he even got his claws into them. Cunningly, rather than stare Bigteef down, Gordrakk engaged him in a yelling contest instead. The noise caused an avalanche to drop a nearby mountaintop on them, after which Gordrakk put a hood over Bigteef's head to claim him. Other orruks say that Gordrakk is so much like Gork that he came with brutality to spare, and one day he wrung the surplus out of his fists and onto the ground, where it grew into Bigteef on the spot.

As powerful as Bigteef is, Gordrakk's true threat to the realms extends beyond the reach of his axes or mount. As the Megaboss of Megabosses, Gordrakk draws all forces that thrive on destruction to him. All orruks flock to fight in his Great Waaagh!, and even grots raise their tiny voices in cries of battle. Gargants, ogors, troggoths and more charge alongside them, adding their power to the destructive violence Gordrakk unleashes. If the Ironjawz are a combative tornado spinning across the Mortal Realms, Gordrakk is standing in its eye.

ORRUK MEGABOSSES

Smashing and stomping everything in reach, the orruk Megabosses lead the Ironjaw warclans with ready violence and brutish cunning. They are the biggest of the Ironjawz, their bodies growing large with muscle until they become icons of destruction at the head of great greenskin crusades.

It is well known among the Ironjawz that the more fights an orruk wins, the bigger they become, their muscles thickening and their teeth getting longer as their body grows. Understandably, then, Megabosses are massive, so huge they overshadow even the mightiest opponents. Some Ironjawz reckon that the reason Megabosses are the biggest is because Gork (or maybe Mork) is inside them, trying to get out. Supposedly, if they get big enough one day, they will become one of the gods themselves and go around punching down mountains or stomping on fortresses. Others say Megabosses have always been the biggest, following the trusted orruk logic of 'it was like that when I found it'.

Ironjaw Megabosses are surpassingly brutal warriors. Whether clanking along on foot, or bawling from the back of a Maw-krusha, they batter down enemies like a landslide of fists. Given their size and peerless combat skills, Megabosses get to wear the heaviest armour and have the biggest choppas. The best bits of iron taken from the battlefield will often find their way to the Megaboss, where he will beat them onto his body, giving his armour its own suit of armour. In addition to layers of the shiniest iron, Megabosses hammer on trophies – the skulls of tough-looking creatures, bits of broken weapons or symbols ripped from the banners of enemies that looked important.

The power of a Megaboss rests in more than just muscle and iron, and as focal points for the Waaagh! they have a bestial charisma that draws other Ironjawz towards them from all directions. The destruction wreaked by a gathering Waaagh! is often almost as bad as the event itself.

Competition between Megabosses is frequent, and often includes headbutting contests, orruk hurling or kill tallies. The latter practice is particularly contentious, as only an exceptional Megaboss can keep track of the numbers involved after the opening moments of a battle. The contest generally devolves into a lot of yelling, and, inevitably, fighting.

MAW-KRUSHAS

Tiny-minded and short-sighted, the thuggish Maw-krushas barrel across the landscape pulverising anything in their way, be it trees, settlements or screaming people. Their bellow is loud enough to rupture organs, pop eyeballs and pulverise bones. They are even capable of a semblance of flight with their stubby wings, though it has been suggested that this is more the result of gravity not wanting to mess with them. Most creatures have the good sense to steer well clear of Maw-krushas, but not the Ironjawz. At first, Maw-krushas were a chance for brave Ironjawz to prove their mettle – often with fatal results. Then, some Megabosses managed to 'tame' a Maw-krusha, either by yelling right back into their face or clambering up on their back where they couldn't reach them and battering them about the head until they submitted. Maw-krushas never truly accept their riders and need constant reminding of who is in charge. Fortunately, the monsters enjoy smashing stuff just as much as Ironjawz do, and can be distracted by a good fight.

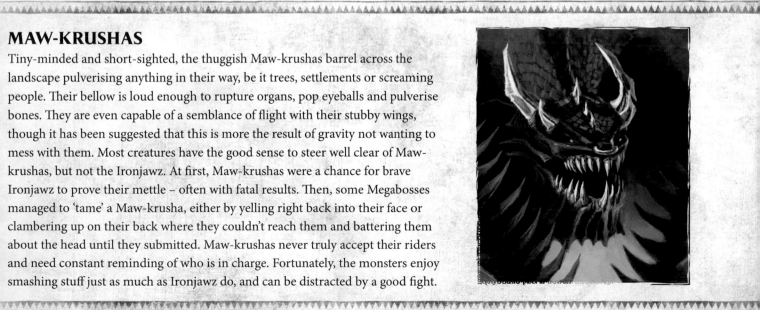

ORRUK WARCHANTERS

The Warchanter's drumming call to war rings out like the constant thunder of ironclad orruks marching across the land. It is a message from the gods summoning the Ironjawz to where the fighting is, and reminding them that Gorkamorka is right there with them every time they start a fight.

Warchanters are the rabble-rousers of the Ironjaw warclans. Crazed followers of Gorkamorka, they hammer out the echoing drumbeat of war with their stikks. The beat calls out to the brutal minds of the Ironjawz and resonates with the energy of the Waaagh!. Driven by the violent rhythm constantly pounding between their ears, a Warchanter will use anything they can to smash out the beat, be it their hitting stikks, bits of mangled iron, enemy skulls or even their fists thumping the faces of their victims. Enemies seldom realise that their screams are adding to the Warchanter's beat.

Every good Megaboss has a Warchanter or two somewhere in their warclan. Whether this is because Megabosses are drawn to the thumping beat of the Warchanter, or the Warchanter is attracted by the thrumming Waaagh! energy of a big boss is unclear, though the effects of this savage union are undeniably effective. Truly impressive Megabosses like Gordrakk, the Fist of Gork, have scores of Warchanters moving amongst their Waaagh!, ensuring that a constant stream of Ironjawz are piling into the boss' force, and every greenskin warrior is riled up and ready for war.

The effects of a Warchanter upon the Ironjawz are terrifying to behold, as hordes of already belligerent orruks stamp their feet and bash their choppas on their armour to the time of the beat, before they hurtle screaming into battle. Such is the mystical nature of the beat that its influence reaches even beyond earshot. Warclans are able to sense the thumping from leagues away, as if it were carried on the wind or vibrating through the ground. For this reason, Warchanters are extremely valuable tools for Megabosses who are trying to replace casualties and grow their warclans.

ORRUK WEIRDNOB SHAMANS

Waaagh! magic is violent and wildly unpredictable, much like the Weirdnobs that harness it. Crackling with the brutal energies spilling off their orruk kin, the shamans shape the Waaagh! into spells, pounding their victims to bloody paste or tearing the battlefield apart like paper.

Weirdnob Shamans are living conduits for the Waaagh!, gifted by Gorkamorka with the power to shape this roiling green energy into calamitous magical effects. Not even the Ironjawz know why some orruks become shamans, though it might have something to do with getting hit really hard on the head – this being the tried and true method of changing an orruk's mind or giving them a really good idea. Lending weight to this theory, Weirdnobs never seem to be completely in control of their bodies, and they twist and twitch as they gibber and stare about with wild eyes or talk to the air.

Other Ironjawz don't normally mess with Weirdnobs. Many are the accounts of bored Brutes poking the brawl shaman with a stick just to see what would happen, only to have their heads violently turned inside out. All orruks know Weirdnobs are crazy, but they are also devastating in a fight, and the bigger the scrap, the more impressive the results of dragging along a Weirdnob. Being too close to one in battle can be dangerous, as orruk heads have a tendency to explode when a Weirdnob unleashes his power. However, Ironjawz consider it worth the risk to see a Weirdnob 'go off'.

Much like the smell of a Weirdnob, Waaagh! spells are almost always offensive in nature. At their most limited, this can be a shower of green fists that pummels enemies into the ground or a wave of crushing force that flattens part of the battlefield like a giant world-grunta has rolled over in its sty. Should enough orruks gather together, a Weirdnob can become so filled with energy they might vomit forth a green river of searing ectoplasmic energy that brings down fortress walls and sweeps away towns, or conjure a foot the size of a mountain to kick an entire army in the face.

ORRUK BRUTES

A thickset brow and heavy iron armour frame the angry stare of an orruk Brute, their mind filled only with violence. Filling out the guts of most Ironjaw warclans, these hulking orruks form a mighty greenskin sledgehammer ready to shatter enemy formations and fortresses to screams of 'Waaagh!'.

Wrapped in iron armour crudely beaten over massive green muscles, Brutes are bigger and meaner than most other warriors of the realms. Brutes are the foot soldiers of the Ironjawz and the most numerous warriors to fight under the clenched fists of the Megabosses. What the Brutes can't beat with violence, they beat with numbers, hacking down their opponents in seemingly endless waves of small-minded aggression. Even hardy creatures like ogors, troggoths or gargants are not safe from the orruks, and as the ancient Brute saying goes, 'if smashing it ain't working, get more boyz to smash it with'.

Ironjaw Brutes know they are the best orruks because they get to do the most fighting. While the Megaboss might do all the pointing and choppa-waving, the Warchanters make some noise, Weirdnobs do all the green magic stuff, and Gore-gruntas think they are the best because they get to go faster, the Brutes are the ones that get things done. When a Megaboss wants to make sure something is smashed 'good and proper' he calls up his Brutefists. Brutes tend to like enemies that hide behind high walls, massive gates or in deep caves, because they don't run away when the Ironjawz show up to give them a kicking. There is also something

small and spiteful in the mind of Brute that doesn't like anything bigger than they are, be it a towering statue of Sigmar, a flaming Magmadroth or a particularly arrogant tree. In battle, which is to say all the time, Brutes seek out these 'big 'uns'. Inevitably, as one Brute spots something worth clobbering a dozen more will join in, not wanting to miss out on the chance to bring it down. More than one beast-riding lord has learned this the hard way, as mobs of Brutes will pile on such lofty warriors in a heaving mountain of green muscle and bad breath until their victim vanishes from sight, much to the horror of their brethren.

Gutrok punched the ghoul's face out the back of its head and into the face of the one behind it. He chuckled darkly to himself even as the ruined head tried to chew on his arm. Gutrok and his boys had stumbled into the nest of ghouls by chance, but now, as the pale creatures spilled from the shadows, they were met by grinning orruks with ready choppas. Then Gutrok spotted a hulking rot-skinned monster.

'Ere, dis one's mine! Any git that gets in my way is going to get himself snipped!'

To drive home his point, Gutrok raised his boss klaw and gave it a grinding snap. Roaring out a battle cry, he charged toward the newcomer. In response, the beast turned glowing red eyes in his direction, giving off a low animal hiss through rows of needle-sharp teeth.

Towering over the boss, the Crypt Horror attacked swiftly, its filthy claws raking down Gutrok's face and side in a shower of blood and sparks. With a crunch of iron, Gutrok brought up his boss klaw and grabbed the beast around its neck. 'Here comes the good bit,' thought Gutrok, oblivious to the blood running down his side or the fact one of his eyes didn't see so good.

'Oi, boss! I fink you need to see dis.'

Gutrok muttered a particularly foul obscenity under his breath as he turned to see a dozen more of the massive horrors ripping their way through his lads. With a gruesome squelch, Gutrok brought his brute smasha down on the horror's head, a shower of putrid blood spattering his armour. Turning back towards the fray, he grinned through the gore and charged.

ORRUK GORE-GRUNTAS

In a tidal wave of porcine flesh, gruntas charge across the battlefield, trampling their victims into the dust and greedily devouring anything they can get their tusks into. On their backs, wild-eyed Ironjawz scream out elated war cries. Together they are Gore-gruntas, the shock troops of the Ironjawz.

Gruntas are massive boar-like beasts with razor-sharp teeth, filthy hides and beady, hate-filled eyes. Notoriously foul-tempered, they are prized mounts for any Ironjawz orruk with the mettle to ride them into battle. Mobs and fists of Gore-gruntas are the shock troops of the Ironjawz, thundering out ahead of any other orruks to get at the foe first. Rusty choppas swung by slab-muscled orruks throw warriors into the air, while the gruntas tear through what's left of the enemy line with their stomping hooves and piercing tusks. Even by the destructive standards of the Ironjawz, a Gore-grunta charge is horrific to behold, especially when entire units vanish under a roaring, grunting mass.

Gruntas will eat practically anything, from the mangled remains of enemies to unobservant orruks, and even the foundations of buildings (they're especially fond of the Khornate ones made out of skulls). Gruntas also eat copious amounts of iron, usually as a result of consuming the more edible things it is attached to, like people. This undigested metal is then harvested by the orruks for weapons and armour and is called pig-iron.

An orruk never really tames a grunta, because the creatures are far too belligerent ever to accept a rider without a fight. When Ironjaw warclans pass through an area where gruntas are known to roam – easily identifiable by the devastation wrought on the local wildlife and landscape, not to mention their copious leavings – some Ironjawz go out on a grunt hunt. Once they have cornered the beasts, orruks hammer bits of iron onto the gruntas, driving the rivets in with their bare fists. This shows they belong to the Ironjawz. It also has the joint benefit of armouring the gruntas and, more importantly, slowing the beasts down just enough to make them possible to ride.

Megabosses prize the Gore-gruntas' ferocity in battle, and know that a well-timed charge can smash apart an enemy army, not to mention make a really satisfying noise as hundreds of snorting monsters pulverise their

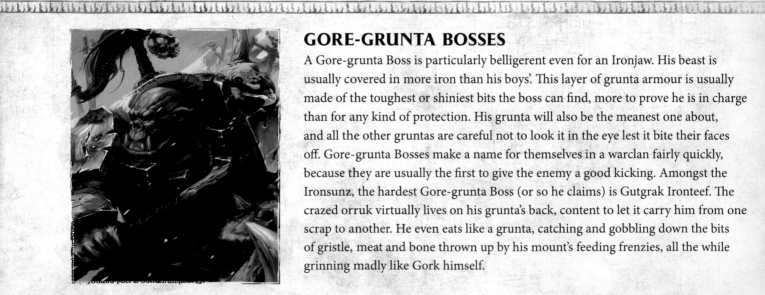

GORE-GRUNTA BOSSES

A Gore-grunta Boss is particularly belligerent even for an Ironjaw. His beast is usually covered in more iron than his boys'. This layer of grunta armour is usually made of the toughest or shiniest bits the boss can find, more to prove he is in charge than for any kind of protection. His grunta will also be the meanest one about, and all the other gruntas are careful not to look it in the eye lest it bite their faces off. Gore-grunta Bosses make a name for themselves in a warclan fairly quickly, because they are usually the first to give the enemy a good kicking. Amongst the Ironsunz, the hardest Gore-grunta Boss (or so he claims) is Gutgrak Ironteef. The crazed orruk virtually lives on his grunta's back, content to let it carry him from one scrap to another. He even eats like a grunta, catching and gobbling down the bits of gristle, meat and bone thrown up by his mount's feeding frenzies, all the while grinning madly like Gork himself.

foes. In countless battles throughout the ages, the Gore-gruntas have been responsible for the most spectacular Ironjaw victories, and the destruction of some of the greatest armies ever to stand against the greenskins.

Cunning bosses have come up with their own vaunted Gore-grunta strategies, like the Tusks of Gork, the Hoof Puncher or the fearsome Snorting Snout Spear. Grunta riders argue endlessly over which tactics are the best for smashing up the enemy, while other orruks point out, at their peril, that they are all basically the same: get a bunch of Gore-gruntas together and charge them into the enemy as fast as they will go.

From time to time, huge grunta migrations thunder across the realms, stirred up by Gorkamorka's war-making, or so the Ironjawz believe. At these auspicious times, warclans send out their bravest or most reckless boys to create a war-sty. Digging out yawning pits, smashing together massive scrap walls or felling entire forests, the orruks build sprawling corrals and drive the grunta herds into them. These seething seas of bristly, lice-ridden hide are then whipped into a frenzy by the Ironjawz. Big rocks, bits of iron and the odd screaming grot are all hurled into the mass until the gruntas are good and angry. The orruks themselves then leap into the mess, each scrambling and grabbing until they manage to mount a grunta.

When the corral gate is finally flung open, what is unleashed is a stampede of snorting violence that tears across the landscape, crashing through anything in its path. Sometimes, grunta herds are of such magnitude that there are enough beasts to carry an entire warclan across the Mortal Realms from one battle to the next.

ORRUK ARDBOYS

Strength calls to strength. Drawn in by the brutal might of the Ironjawz are countless Ardboy mobs. Among the strongest of the other orruks, Ardboys flock to the brawls of the hulking Ironjawz, eager to prove themselves to a Megaboss with acts of bone-crunching violence.

To orruks, the Ironjawz are like the fists of Gorkamorka pounding the face of the Mortal Realms. Ardboys hear this thundering tempo of violence and abandon their tribes to fight at the side of these mightiest of greenskins. Of all the other orruks, Ardboys are the only ones that are tolerated in the Ironjaw warclans, for they are the hardest boys about – next to the Ironjawz themselves.

Already great warriors themselves, the Ardboys seek to make themselves harder still, plastering themselves in armour and toting massive choppas in imitation of the Ironjawz. Despite their prodigious strength, enough to break the spine of a man one-handed,

they cannot beat iron into shape with their hands like the Ironjawz. Instead, they forge it from salvaged iron, displaying surprising skill for their race, and giving their mobs a distinctive appearance.

Ardboys form their own mobs and fists within the Ironjaw warclans. Strangely for orruks, they believe in discipline and have banners and drums so they can fight in ranks or march about in lines. Blazoned across the Ardboys' banners are images of horned and iron-jawed orruks, perhaps representing how the Ardboys see themselves, or to depict the Ironjawz they follow to war. They also give their fists fearsome names like the Facesmashas or the

Gutrippas, to make them seem even harder. Most Ironjawz think Ardboys are a bit funny – after all, what's marching to a drum got to do with smashing skulls – but admit that they know their stuff when it comes to war.

Eager to impress the Ironjawz, Ardboys fight all the harder when there is a Megaboss about. If there is a tough job to do, Ardboys mobs are often the first to charge forward to do it, scaling fortress walls, hunting down enemy lords or braving deadly terrain. Rivalry between Ardboys mobs is also common, and fists of Ardboys thunder into the fray, smashing and bashing everything in sight, each mob eager to prove they are the best.

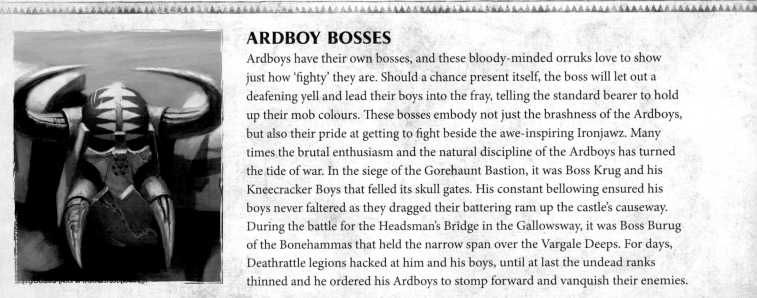

ARDBOY BOSSES

Ardboys have their own bosses, and these bloody-minded orruks love to show just how 'fighty' they are. Should a chance present itself, the boss will let out a deafening yell and lead their boys into the fray, telling the standard bearer to hold up their mob colours. These bosses embody not just the brashness of the Ardboys, but also their pride at getting to fight beside the awe-inspiring Ironjawz. Many times the brutal enthusiasm and the natural discipline of the Ardboys has turned the tide of war. In the siege of the Gorehaunt Bastion, it was Boss Krug and his Kneecracker Boys that felled its skull gates. His constant bellowing ensured his boys never faltered as they dragged their battering ram up the castle's causeway. During the battle for the Headsman's Bridge in the Gallowsway, it was Boss Burug of the Bonehammas that held the narrow span over the Vargale Deeps. For days, Deathrattle legions hacked at him and his boys, until at last the undead ranks thinned and he ordered his Ardboys to stomp forward and vanquish their enemies.

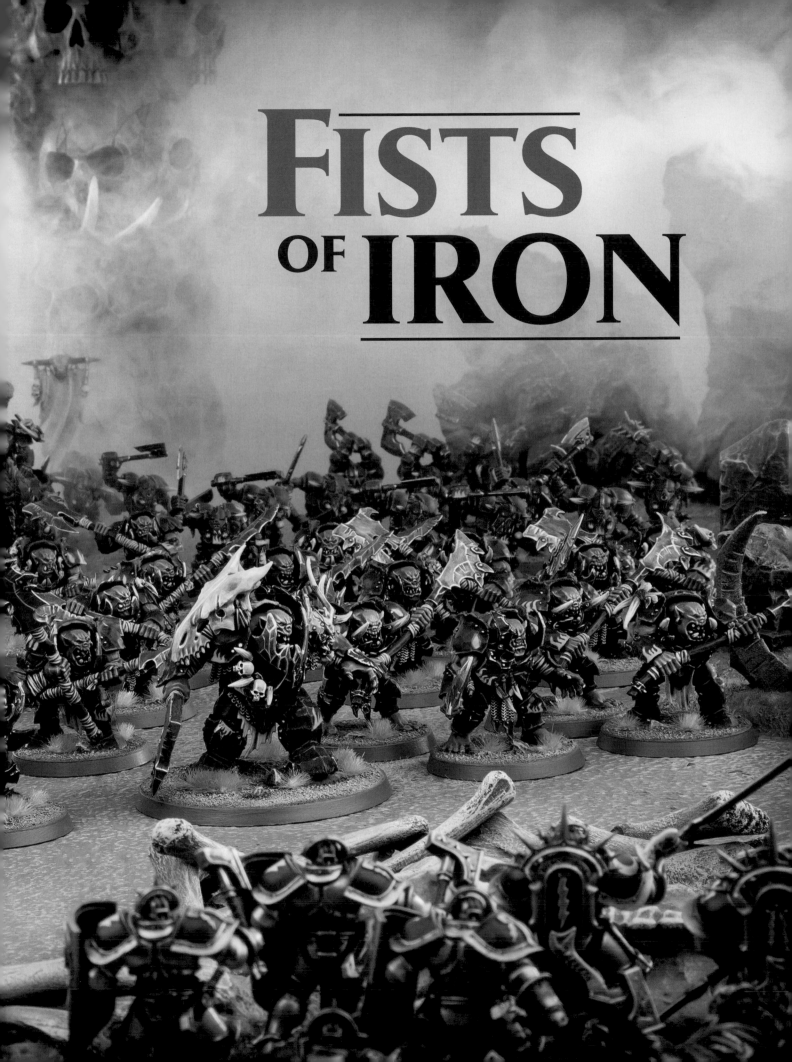

FISTS
OF IRON

The power of Gorkamorka courses through both Weirdnob Shamans and Warchanters.

The ground shudders under the thundering hooves of an Ironjaw Gore-grunta mob.

Gore-gruntas crush and trample anything in their way in their eagerness to get to the fight.

Weirdnob Shamans channel and unleash the destructive Waaagh! energy generated by frenzied orruks.

Orruk Brutes are hulking fighters who live solely to smash, stomp and kill.

Warchanters pound the rhythm of war on anything in reach – including the enemy.

Orruk Megaboss

Orruk Weirdnob Shaman

Orruk Warchanter

Orruk Brute

Orruk Brute Boss

Orruk Brute

Orruk Gore-grunta

Orruk Gore-grunta

Orruk Gore-grunta Boss

Orruk 'Gore-grunta

Orruk Brute   **Orruk Brute Boss**   **Orruk Brute**

Megaboss on Maw-krusha

Gordrakk, the Fist of Gork

REALMS OF WAAAGH!

THE GREAT WAAAGH!

The thunderous tumult of war is calling to the Ironjawz. As battle spreads across the Mortal Realms, their warclans gather in numbers not seen in an age, roused into a stampede of destruction that seeks only to knock down and stomp into the dust everything in its path.

During the Age of Chaos, the Ironjawz fought endless wars against the minions of the Dark Gods. It was a glorious time for the greenskins, one of continuous bloodshed and face-kicking. Many legendary Chaos lords like Jarrak Voidheart and the Razored Queen, Aberleth, sought to destroy the ironclad orruk warclans in this time. Impregnable fortresses, daemon armies that blanketed the land and horrific spells of extermination were all set against the Ironjawz; but they all met with failure. A lord would declare they had conquered a kingdom and subdued its creatures in the name of the Dark

Gods, only for an Ironjaw warclan to thunder out of the wilds and destroy everything in its path. As war spread like a contagion across the Mortal Realms, many races and kingdoms found themselves caught between the insidious domain of Chaos and the wanton destruction of the Ironjawz.

Most importantly for the Ironjaw warclans, this age of war without end made them strong. There was always plenty of iron to loot, and all the fighting gave rise to some of the greatest Megabosses ever to stomp their way across the realms.

In this time, the Ironjawz were at their strongest in the kingdoms of Ghur, though their warclans could be found throughout the realms stirring up trouble. From the Realm of Beasts many a great Waaagh! wrought a path of destruction under the leadership of a powerful Megaboss. By their nature, wars conducted by Ironjaw bosses were more destructive than those led by other greenskins, the ironclad Megabosses able to muster the biggest orruks around and keep them together for longer. The cave peoples of Ascandia and the dreg-kings of the Murmarsh still whisper legends of

the Iron Orruks as they huddle in the ruins of their once-great empires. Like the ebb and flow of a green tide, each Waaagh! grew from the violence of a handful of warclans until it crashed down upon the realms with punishing force. Great Waaagh! after Great Waaagh! rolled across the ages like an avalanche, and like the Ironjawz' thirst for destruction, they were never-ending. As the Age of Sigmar dawns across the Mortal Realms, this cycle is set to repeat itself. Already the Ironjawz can see the signs – suns that rise burning green, mountains that rumble and belch out orruk war cries, and the image of Gorkamorka grinning at them from the storm clouds. According to the Weirdnob Shamans, one of the five mystical portents of the Great Waaagh! has already come to pass: the rise of the Fist of Gork, the Megaboss that will lead the clans to war.

As the Great Waaagh! builds, the Ironjawz have been wreaking havoc throughout the Mortal Realms. Spoiling the strategies of all sides, Ironjaw warclans ambush armies on the march, strike against remote garrisons and attack forces already locked in battle. Perhaps most dangerous of all, they seek out Realmgates, knowing that there will be ample foes to fight through the mystical gates. Across the realms, many commanders have looked to Realmgates for their reinforcements, only to be greeted by an ear-splitting 'Waaagh!' and the sight of thousands of savage Ironjawz thundering out toward them. Bloodbound Warhordes, Stormcast Eternal Stormhosts and countless other armies have all met their end at the hands of the Ironjawz in this way, and blow by blow the orruks have changed the face of the Realmgate Wars.

Just as the plans of many commanders in the field have suffered under the orruks' indiscriminate actions, so too have garrisons, keeps and cities been wiped away by the storm of violence to leave only smoking ruins and corpses behind. More than one general has sought refuge from their foes only to discover leering greenskins looking down at them from their own battlements, or standing proudly over the heap of rubble that was once an allied kingdom.

While Slann Starmasters, Lord-Celestants and the finest commanders to grace the realms might ponder at the tactics of the Ironjawz, the greenskins give it altogether less thought. Where there is war the brawls gather, and where there are enemies to pound into the ground there will be a Megaboss ready to do the pounding.

THE RIVER OF SOULS

Queen Aylessa's barge-keep carved a path through the Nightlands as it drifted along a river of spirits, and the vampire surveyed the lands she ruled. Then came the sound of drumming, and ten thousand roaring Ironjaw voices carried on the wind, all bellowing for Aylessa's head.

Out of the Arch of Secrets spilled the Ironsunz. Their Megaboss, Dakkbad Grotkicker, was the first to bull his way into the Nightlands of Shyish. Snuffling the air, mobs of Gore-gruntas followed, then clanking, cursing mobs of Brutes all looking to Dakkbad to tell them where the fighting was. Narrowing his eyes, the Megaboss looked out across the rolling landscape of haunted ruins and crumbling cities toward a glowing river that flickered and danced in the darkness with thousands of writhing ghosts. This was the way his Weirdnob

Shaman had said Megaboss Grugek and his Brokeknuckle Boyz had gone – and Dakkbad had some unfinished business with Grugek. With a grunt, the Megaboss led his warclan into the Nightlands looking for a scrap.

On the edge of the River of Souls sprawled the decaying city of Crookback, its skeletal inhabitants toiling mindlessly at their tasks. With a teeth-shaking Waaagh!, Dakkbad and his Maw-krusha Skullzcrakka hurtled into the city, thousands of

Ironjawz charging in behind them. At once, legions of Deathrattle warriors shambled to defend their town, and in a shower of splintered bone and orruk blood the two armies crashed together. At the fore, Dakkbad ploughed through enemies and buildings with disdain, leaving a great furrow of destruction behind him. Brutes rained choppa and smasha blows down on skeletal bodies, while rusting weapons thrust back to pierce green hides. On the flanks Gore-gruntas rolled through the enemy, the beasts' mouths stuffed with bones.

With plodding determination, the Deathrattle forces moved to blunt the Ironjawz' charge. Creaking siege-gates were hauled into place, and fleshless archers lined the tops of skull-studded towers as pale-faced Deathmages summoned up fresh corpses to bar the orruks' way. However, each strongpoint was brought down in turn, the Ironjawz simply throwing their weight at foundations and supports until, with screams of tortured wood and stone, the buildings crashed down to become naught but dust and rubble.

From the upper decks of her mighty barge-keep, Aylessa watched the Ironjawz smashing the grand city of Crookback to pieces and snarled, showing alabaster fangs. With a wave of her hand, she loosed her Morghast attendants and murderous spirits to deal with the savage invaders. Flying and floating on an ethereal wind above a causeway of roiling spirits, Aylessa's forces advanced on the besieged city.

Dakkbad hefted his choppa to hack apart another dead thing only to discover that there was nothing but broken bones beneath Skullzcrakka's fists. Nearby, the remains of the city's skeletal defenders were still fighting, but howling Brutes and snorting Gore-gruntas were stomping on them from all sides. Most of the city was now lying in tangled, broken ruins. Then, from out of the dark skies, wailing ranks of undead appeared. First came the Morghasts, striking the Ironjaw brawl like a punishing spear thrust. Second came the wraiths, with their grinning skulls and witchfire-filled eye sockets. Many generals might have been wrong-footed by these newcomers, but Dakkbad's face split with a toothy grin, his disappointment of a moment ago washed away by the impending violence. Despite the Megaboss' joy, however, the Ironjawz were now being forced back, where only seconds before they had owned the field. Massive winged Morghasts hacked orruks apart

with blinding speed, while the death-cursed scythes of the Cairn Wraiths turned flesh to dust with each chilling swing. A wave of uncertainty passed through the orruks, and for a moment, the fate of the battle hung in the balance. Then the drumbeat began.

All through the battle, Warchanter Borguz had been hammering with his stikks, but now he picked up the tempo, his frenzy infecting the nearby orruks. Even then, it might not have been enough to turn the tide against the terrifying undead, had not the haunted lands surrounding the city come alive with Ardboys. Heeding Borguz's call, they poured into the ruins, coming from the orruk tribes of the Nightlands to join the Ironjawz. Dakkbad slammed into the monstrous Morghasts, scattering their winged formation, his army answering the undead's fury tenfold until nothing remained of the city but ash, splinters and the retreating remnants of Aylessa's army.

DAKKBAD GROTKICKER

Dakkbad Grotkicker is as cunning as a double-edged choppa. Part of Gordrakk's Megafist, he is one of the Fist of Gork's Megabosses. Dakkbad's own warclan, the Ironsunz, are always at the forefront of Gordrakk's growing Waaagh! where the fighting is toughest. Dakkbad has earned the name Grotkicker for his underhanded, even sneaky, plans. The Megaboss has been exerting his dominance over the other bosses in the Megafist, trying to prove he is the best orruk to stand at Gordrakk's side. During his rise, he has maimed dozens of other bosses. His favoured tactic is to collect their fingers when he takes their boys, feeding the green digits to his Maw-krusha Skullzcrakka. Most recently, Dakkbad has been looking for the Megaboss Grugek, after Grugek made off with his favourite boss choppa. At least, Dakkbad thinks it was one of his – boss choppas have a habit of looking quite similar. Either way, he plans to have some 'words' with Grugek and get back that choppa – or carve a new one out of Grugek's armour.

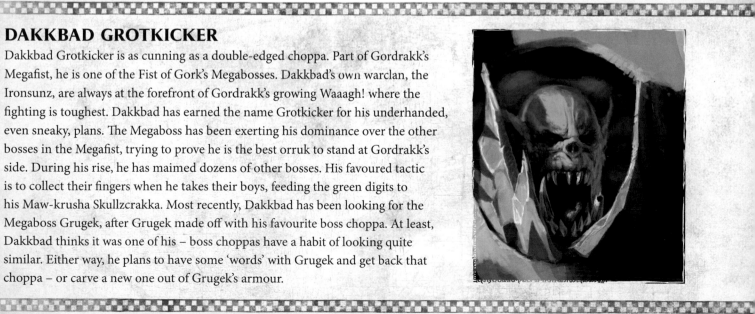

Dakkbad brought his fist down onto the massive skull of the last Morghast. The creature took two or three more good thumps before it stopped moving about. Looking up at where the undead had come from, he spotted what looked like a giant floating castle sailing down the river of glowy stuff.

'Right ladz, that's where Grugek's boyz must 'ave gone, it's the only fing round here worth smashing.' With a grunt, Dakkbad noticed that no one was listening – his boys were still wrecking the city and chasing the last of the dead things about.

'*OI! YOU GITS!*' Dakkbad bellowed at the top of his lungs. A number of nearby Brutes were staggered by the deafening blast. To his satisfaction, the rest of the brawl were now looking in his direction, even if a few of the boys were still idly stomping on things. Giving Skullzcrakka a kick, Dakkbad started off in the direction of the ship-thing, when one of his boys ran up.

'Boss, that glowy stuff don't look right, how are we going to get across it?'

Dakkbad gave a broken-toothed grin. 'I'm the boss, you leave that to me.'

For days of ceaseless twilight, the Ironjawz followed Aylessa's vessel down the River of Souls. The vampire set desperate ambushes in the dead cities they passed in an effort to slow the horde, but her spectral hosts fell as before, and the cities crumbled under jagged-edged choppas. Yet, as satisfying as this destruction was for Dakkbad, it was just part of the Megaboss' cunning plan. While Aylessa's eyes were fixed on the Ironsunz' rampage, Dakkbad's Gore-gruntas had ranged out ahead of the brawl to something the Nightlands Ardboys had told the boss about. As the barge-keep rounded a twist in the river, the monolithic Deathlord's Gate loomed up above it, a towering statue of Nagash that stood astride the river. At Dakkbad's signal, the Gore-gruntas battered at the legs of the statue, and the edifice plunged into the river before Aylessa's keep, driving it to the bank.

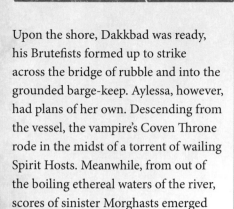

Upon the shore, Dakkbad was ready, his Brutefists formed up to strike across the bridge of rubble and into the grounded barge-keep. Aylessa, however, had plans of her own. Descending from the vessel, the vampire's Coven Throne rode in the midst of a torrent of wailing Spirit Hosts. Meanwhile, from out of the boiling ethereal waters of the river, scores of sinister Morghasts emerged and swept into the orruks' ranks.

Dakkbad plunged into the undead ranks, causing the spectral army to part around his Maw-krusha as he tromped toward the Coven Throne. Nearby, shaking statue dust from their fur, Gore-gruntas swept around to face the Morghasts. However, as the beasts drew close to the edge of the river, they grew even more unruly, snorting furiously as Spirit Hosts reached out of the waters toward them. The bone monsters turned from scything their way through mobs of Ardboys to face the Gorefists, the two sides smashing together to a riot of wild snorts and spine-chilling howls. Then, from the midst of the Morghasts emerged a willowy figure. Opening her mouth impossibly wide, the Banshee let out a heart-stopping scream. In that instant, dozens of orruks and gruntas crashed to the ground, their flesh turning pale as the life was stolen from them. Over the corpses, the tide of undead continued its charge, decimating Dakkbad's Brutes.

The Megaboss and Maw-krusha hit the vampire's throne like a cannonball. Spirits scattered and Aylessa's coven was thrown to the ground, splinters showering in all directions. A pale blur, Aylessa leapt clear, all grace and death. Her flashing blade carved a deep furrow down Dakkbad's armour, but he barely noticed. Skullzcrakka stamped through Aylessa's brood, and the only hissing vampire to clamber up the Maw-krusha's side was met by a face-shattering headbutt from Dakkbad.

On the ground, amid the ruins of her Coven Throne, Aylessa was a whirlwind of murder, holding back a dozen Brutes. The Megaboss looked over the melee and saw the Morghasts caving in the side of his army, as more spirits emerged from the river to join them. The fearsome Morghasts had been unexpected, but Dakkbad had an idea. Turning Skullzcrakka from the fight, he swooped over the undead host toward the side of the vessel that lay beneath the waterline. Plunging into the river, the Maw-krusha punched a hole in its hull. Screaming out in rage, Aylessa turned her army from slaughtering the orruks to try to save her ship. But she was too late. By the time the vampire had fought her way onto the deck, the ship was already sliding back, beneath the ghostly waters. As the last darkly graceful spire vanished into the river, she saw Dakkbad upon the shore leering at her from the back of his beast, the orruk's brutish laughter booming out into the Nightlands.

AYLESSA, CONSORT OF THE BLOOD QUEEN

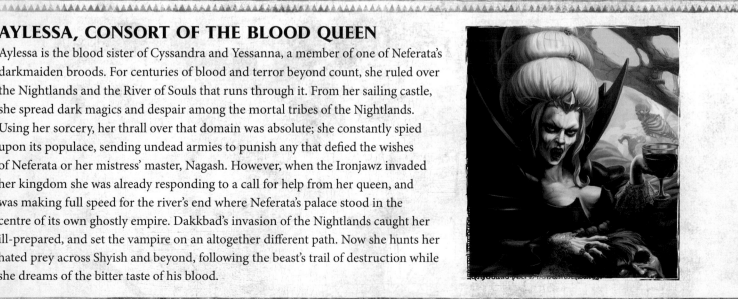

Aylessa is the blood sister of Cyssandra and Yessanna, a member of one of Neferata's darkmaiden broods. For centuries of blood and terror beyond count, she ruled over the Nightlands and the River of Souls that runs through it. From her sailing castle, she spread dark magics and despair among the mortal tribes of the Nightlands. Using her sorcery, her thrall over that domain was absolute; she constantly spied upon its populace, sending undead armies to punish any that defied the wishes of Neferata or her mistress' master, Nagash. However, when the Ironjawz invaded her kingdom she was already responding to a call for help from her queen, and was making full speed for the river's end where Neferata's palace stood in the centre of its own ghostly empire. Dakkbad's invasion of the Nightlands caught her ill-prepared, and set the vampire on an altogether different path. Now she hunts her hated prey across Shyish and beyond, following the beast's trail of destruction while she dreams of the bitter taste of his blood.

HOW TO USE BATTLEPLANS

This book contains three battleplans, each of which enables you to fight a battle based upon the exciting narrative that leads up to it. These battles should be fought using all of the rules on the *Warhammer Age of Sigmar* rules sheet unless the battleplan specifically indicates otherwise. Each of the battleplans includes a map reflecting the landscape on which the battle was fought; these maps usually show a battlefield that is 6 feet by 4 feet in size, but you can use a smaller or larger area if you wish.

The only thing that Ironjawz love more than a good fight is to inflict total, wanton destruction. Any foe faced by a rampaging Ironjaw horde has little option but to stand and fight. Attempting to flee will only result in the destruction of all they hold dear, and in any case, the Ironjawz will eventually track them to their hiding place and force them to do battle anyway. This leaves the defenders no choice but to defeat the Ironjawz before they have penetrated too far into their homeland. With luck, they will drive the greenskins back before the Ironjawz can reduce everything to a blasted wilderness.

THE ARMIES

One player commands an Ironjawz army, and the other commands the protectors of the territory that the Ironjawz have invaded.

IRONJAWZ' OBJECTIVES

You and your boys have been looking for a good fight for ages and have, at last, found an opponent willing to put up a fight. What is more, they seem determined to protect some of their puny buildings and idols from you and your lads. The prospect of a good punch-up *and* the chance to inflict a bit of mindless destruction has filled you with glee, and you can hardly wait to get stuck in. You will wreck all of the stupid landmarks they are trying to protect, and leave nothing but burning ruins behind you. With a loud 'Waaagh!' you lead the boys into battle.

PROTECTOR'S OBJECTIVES

The Ironjaw horde that confronts you has already rampaged across several neighbouring territories. Judging by the clouds of smoke that have marked their progress, they are leaving nothing standing when they move on. It is unthinkable to you that they inflict the same sort of carnage upon your kingdom, and so you have determined that you must stop them here, right at the border to your lands. You will either annihilate the greenskin destroyers, or die in the attempt!

PROTECTOR'S COMMAND ABILITY

The protector's general has the following command ability, in addition to any others that they have.

A Living Bulwark: If the general uses this ability, then they and all units from their army within 15" form a protective barrier. The general and these units cannot move until the next hero phase, but until then, you can add 1 to all hit and save rolls for those units. In addition, until then, IRONJAWZ units cannot move to within 6" of any units in the living bulwark unless they are making a charge or pile in move, and any that are between 3" and 6" from any units in the bulwark can only retreat or charge.

THE BATTLEFIELD

The battle takes place on the border of the protector's kingdom.

You will need at least six terrain features in order to use this battleplan. Set them up so that at least half are within the area of the battlefield in which the protectors will deploy. These pieces of terrain represent the locations that the protectors are defending from the Ironjaw horde.

SET-UP

The Ironjawz set up first, with all models within 12" of one of the narrow edges of the battlefield. The protectors set up second, anywhere that is more than 18" from the Ironjawz' territory.

FIRST TURN

The Ironjawz take the first turn in the first round of the battle.

SPECIAL TERRAIN RULES

A number of special rules apply to the terrain features located in the protector's territory:

VANDALISM

The Ironjawz are determined both to destroy the protectors and also smash apart all of the terrain features that the protectors are trying to defend. To represent this, units from the Ironjawz army can vandalise terrain features in the protector's territory.

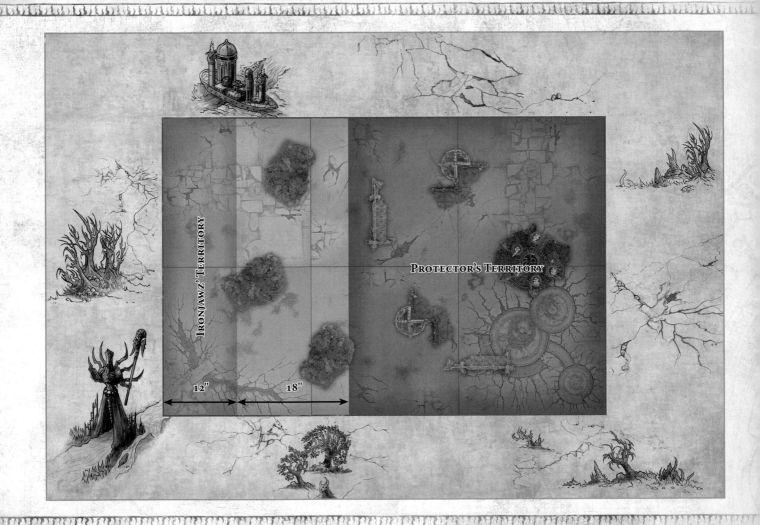

The Ironjawz can attempt to vandalise a terrain feature if there are any Ironjawz models in or on the feature in their hero phase. Both players roll a dice and add the number of models they have in or on the feature to the dice roll. If the Ironjawz player rolls higher, then the feature has been vandalised!

In addition, one Weirdnob Shaman in the Ironjawz army knows the Gorkamorka Stomp! spell, in addition to any other spells that they know. The Ironjawz player should say which Weirdnob Shaman knows the spell when they are set up.

THE GORKAMORKA STOMP!
The Gorkamorka Stomp! has a casting value of 7. If successfully cast, pick a terrain feature within 12" of the caster, and roll two dice. If the total rolled on the dice is equal to or greater than

the distance between the caster and the terrain feature, then it is treated as having been vandalised (see left).

VICTORY
Do not use any of the victory conditions on the *Warhammer Age of Sigmar* rules sheet. Instead, the player commanding the Ironjawz wins a **major victory** if they can vandalise more than half of the terrain features in the protector's deployment area before the end of the fifth battle round. If they fail to do so then the protector wins a **major victory**.

In addition, either side wins a **major victory** if the opposing army is destroyed and there are no enemy models left on the field of battle.

HINTS & TIPS
This battleplan works best if the Ironjawz army slightly outnumbers the protectors, but doesn't have an overwhelming advantage. We also recommend that you set up an odd number of terrain features in the protector's territory; we have found that either 3 or 5 pieces is ideal, depending on the size of each player's army. Finally, you should only use fortifications if the protector is heavily outnumbered by the Ironjawz and needs a little bit of help; the intent of this battleplan is that the protectors defend the scenery, rather than hide inside it!

ACROSS THE WORLD CHASM

Smoke from the Salishwyrd Cities blotted out the sky, as clouds rose from burning arboreal fortresses. At the edge of the World Chasm, where two impossibly vast continents almost touched, the Bloodtoofs Warclan paused, the vast barrier having halted their rampage across sylvaneth lands.

Zectoka gazed down from the stars above the Jade Realm, his ancient eyes following the path of destruction wrought by the Ironjawz. Even to look upon the wild orruks was painful for the slann, as their destructive existence frayed the fates and made all futures they touched unpredictable. The slann had watched while the Yewood Kingdoms had fallen, believing that the rest of the Living Plains would remain safe, as they were protected by the World Chasm. The slann's expectation was that the ever-fractious Ironjawz, denied any other opponents, would turn on each other, tearing themselves apart in their unending lust for battle. He saw, however, that once again the orruks had proven his predictions wrong. The Ironjawz were attacking the roots of the tree city of Silverglade with wild abandon. It did not take a great mind to understand their crude plan. The time had come to act.

Stepping out of the ether, the slann materialised upon the creaking oaken crossing. Far below, a river of worlds' blood glowed like a ribbon of flame, promising a swift end to any that fell into the chasm. Megaboss Zogbak clambered up onto the huge fallen tree. Behind him, his Bloodtoofs were still smashing apart the castle-sized roots of the Silverglade Oak, cutting down the few remaining Branchwraiths to crawl out of the loamy ruin. Up ahead, across the chasm, a new land awaited. Zogbak rubbed his toothy jaw in anticipation of the fighting to come. Yelling out to his Brutefists, Zogbak stalked out onto the bridge, its surface covered with a forest of huge, tangled branches.

Zogbak slammed into the last tree-thing, sending it spinning off the edge of the cliff in a shower of splinters. The Megaboss spat over the edge after it, thinking they were hardly worth the trouble.

Looking up, Zogbak considered the huge gulf that separated the scorched ground on which he stood, his back to the burning tree city, and the green lands on the far side. 'Dat's a grottin' shame,' he muttered. It didn't seem right that Gork should give them all these kingdoms to duff up only to put a stonking great hole between him and more scrapping.

'Ere boss.' One of his boys ran up, urgently pointing behind him.

'Not now, yer git, I'z tryin' to figure out how to get across this hole.'

'But Boss...'

Zogbak was about to remind the orruk why he was the boss when there was a mighty roar of ripping wood. Like an Aleguzzler trying to step over a river, the mile-high oak came crashing down, narrowly missing the Megaboss, to form a bridge across the gulf. 'Right, I've figured it out,' bellowed Zogbak, 'let's cross this fing!'

From between the boughs, cerulean light suddenly erupted; rays like ghostly spears stabbing toward the sky. Zectoka's seraphon army materialised across the surface of the tree bridge, a wall of roaring celestial warriors and hulking reptilian beasts. Zogbak didn't even hesitate – with a mighty bellow, the Megaboss charged toward the defenders before they had any chance to ready their lines, and his army charged after him, spurred on by the chance for a fresh scrap so soon after smashing up the sylvaneth. Snorting, Zogbak's Gorefists broke into the lead, crashing through the branches like a tsunami even as Saurus Warriors tried to block their way.

Without breaking stride, hundreds of Gore-gruntas barrelled into the saurus lines to the thunderous roar of hooves and bawling Ironjawz. As they passed, seraphon were hurled into the air or flung into the void that stretched to either side of the bridge. Scaled muscle tried to hold back rampaging beast-flesh, but the orruk charge could not be denied. Amid the carnage, Zogbak arrived, laying about himself with his massive boss choppa, each swing felling ranks of hissing foes. The seraphon moved swiftly to contain the breakthrough by the Gore-gruntas. On the flanks, swarms of skinks rained celestial missiles down onto the orruk riders, while from the sky Terradons swooped low, hurling rocks into the fray. However, it was akin to throwing pebbles at a charging troggoth.

Zectoka, ringed by his Saurus Guard, did not flinch as his army parted like flesh before an iron blade. Instead, he called out to the stars, weaving magics both ancient and terrible into a deadly spell. Meteors fell from the sky, each one hurtling down to punch through the oak in a shower of splintered wood and flame. Burning gruntas squealed in pain as they and their riders were thrown into the air, plummeting off into the chasm below. The tree began to buckle under the celestial onslaught, creaking and cracking alarmingly as holes appeared in its length. The arrival of thousands of Brutes was certainly not helping matters, even if they were now hewing their way into the seraphon lines. Beyond the rain of blazing comets, Zogbak could see the slann casting his sorceries, and plunged

towards him through the press of slashing blades and snapping fangs. At once, enemies swarmed around him, and it was all he could do just to stop the seraphon from heaving him into the abyss.

Seeing his boss' predicament, Weirdnob Zzapdak stumbled forward, unleashing the power of the Waaagh! in a wave of green, sorcerous energy. Zectoka reached out with his mind and tried to unravel the spell. What should have been as easy as sweeping away a spider's web, however, was more like wading through a writhing pit of worms. Although his opponent was undisciplined, the sheer power the Weirdnob was wielding almost overwhelmed the Starmaster, and the slann had to redouble his efforts.

SALISHWYRD CITIES

POOLS OF TRANQUILITY

REMAINS OF THE YEWOOD

SILVERGLADE CITADEL

WORLD CHASM

LIVING PLAINS

JEWELFLOW POOLS

While slann and Weirdnob struggled over the power of the Waaagh!, Zogbak pressed forward through the mess of combat. Where moments before the bridge had been one side of a vast fallen tree, its branches a forest through which the battle raged, now it was a splintered wasteland, as dozens of yawning holes cracked open in the bark underfoot. Every moment, another rank of saurus or a mob of Brutes tumbled out of sight, and the bridge lurched as it sank another few feet toward breaking.

Battle lines had vanished, Brutefists and Gorefists bulling their way through stubborn Saurus Warriors as skinks moved like shadows through the branch-wood to deal death with javelin and dart. Here and there massive Stegadons and Bastiladons held their own against vicious greenskin charges, but Ironjaw warriors continued to converge on the beasts, eager to claim a great trophy.

At last, the Megaboss reached the far end of the bridge and the ranks of Zectoka's Saurus Guard, a wall of celestite blades raised to bar his way. The Megaboss didn't even slow down, smashing seraphon bodies into bursts of celestial light. Polearms reached out for Zogbak from all sides, most sparking off his armour, and the others brushed aside by sweeps of his choppa.

Though he was locked in sorcerous combat, the slann turned a part of his mind to the Megaboss. Blinding white lightning leapt from Zectoka's palanquin, the bolts of energy arching into the Megaboss and his boys. For a moment, Zogbak's armour danced with blue and silver sparks. Smoke coiling from his mouth and eyes, Zogbak roared. In answer to the yell, those Brutes still standing let out a skull-bursting bellow of their own, and redoubled their assault. Before the onslaught, dozens of Saurus Guard were destroyed, their bodies

punched apart or stomped into the ground. Upon his throne, Zectoka was rudely slapped back into reality, his concentration broken. Zzapdak suddenly found all resistance gone, and like a river bursting through a shattered dam, the power of the Waaagh! was released. A huge green fist erupted from the Weirdnob's mouth, arcing over the fray to come plunging down in the middle of the battle, obliterating hundreds of seraphon. Unfortunately it also finished off the bridge, and with a final crack, the span broke, hurling the combatants in all directions. The slann fled into the ether with a flash, while Zogbak lunged for the ground on the far side. As the two sections of the oak sagged and finally fell into the chasm, the Megaboss found himself with a handful of boys and gruntas on one side, with the rest of his army stuck on the other side. With a dismissive grunt, Zogbak turned toward the unspoilt lands ahead, and set off with his boys to find some trouble.

SLANN STARMASTER ZECTOKA

The Slann Starmaster Zectoka has waged war against the minions of Khorne for years beyond counting. Recently, this sprawling conflict has led the slann into the rotting kingdoms and plague-riddled continents of Ghyran, where Khorne's forces are striving to prevent Nurgle's ascendence. In the foetid swamps and infected vales of the realm, his armies excel at sudden, blazing strikes, vanquishing the enemy before vanishing like dew. For these tactics, Zectoka favours skink cohorts, sometimes summoning thousands of the nimble warriors to lay complex and deadly ambushes for the crazed followers of the Blood God. However, the coming of the Ironjawz has torn apart the slann's carefully laid war plans. As a fire spreads without concern for what it burns, so too have the Ironjawz ripped their way from one arboreal kingdom to the next. With the deliberate determination of the moving heavens, Zectoka is realising that his war against the followers of Khorne will be all the harder if he cannot find a way to blunt the brutal advance of the Ironjawz.

Ironjawz are not noted for either their subtlety or restraint. As often as not, they will charge straight at any enemy they come across, the orruk warriors at the front keen to beat up the foe before the boys at the back can catch up and steal some of their fun. Crashing into the startled enemy, the greenskins will cleave through the centre of the enemy line, and then either carry on rampaging away into the distance, or turn around and smash through them again!

The enemy will have little time to react to this savage onslaught. Their best option is to weather the initial storm, and – if their line can hold – draw in reinforcements from either flank to first contain and then surround and destroy the green horde. However, this is far more easily said than done, and more often the survivors of a defending army will find themselves standing dumbfounded as the Ironjawz rampage off into the distance.

THE ARMIES

One player commands an Ironjawz army, and the other commands a defending army that the Ironjawz have just encountered.

Each army has a unique rule, as shown below.

IRONJAWZ' OBJECTIVES

Until a few moments ago, you were leading your boys on a march into enemy territory. Then some of the lads you had sent ahead returned to say that there was an enemy army blocking your path. Barging the scouts to one side, you paused only long enough to wave your choppa in the right direction, and then you were off in a headlong charge towards the foe. After all, if you aren't quick, some other git might get to them before you do! Behind you, you can hear the cheerful shouts of 'Waaagh!' and ''Ere we go!' as your army follows you into battle. With luck you will be able to smash straight through the enemy line and be on your way again before they know what's hit them.

DEFENDER'S OBJECTIVES

You have been ordered by your lord and master to stop the rampaging Ironjaw horde that is heading towards you. You have deployed your army along their line of march, and spotted their outriders as they crested a nearby rise. You had expected that your opponent would spend some time formulating a plan of battle, but the sound of thundering feet and hooves just beyond the horizon indicates that the greenskins are going to attack immediately. You quickly start to redeploy your army to block the Ironjaw attack. The greenskins must not break through your battle line!

QUICK LADZ, FOLLOW ME!

If the Ironjawz army general is going to make a charge in your charge phase, they must be the first model you roll for. However, when you do so, you can add 2 to their charge roll. In addition, if they make a successful charge, add 2 to the charge rolls of all other units from their army for the rest of that charge phase.

REDEPLOY!

If a unit from the defender's army runs, you can double the run rolls for the unit if it is within 18" of the defender's army general when the roll is made.

THE BATTLEFIELD

The battle takes place where a narrow pathway meets an open plain. The Ironjawz start deployed on the pathway and the defenders on the plain just in front of them. Just beyond the defenders lies an area of open ground that the Ironjawz wish to reach.

Generate the scenery for the battle as described on the *Warhammer Age of Sigmar* rules sheet.

SET-UP

The Ironjawz set up first, anywhere in their territory that is more than 12" from the defender's territory.

The defenders set up second, anywhere in their territory. No more than half of the models in the defending army can be set up in the central 2' by 2' area of their territory (see the map).

FIRST TURN

The Ironjawz take the first turn in the first battle round.

FIRST TURN CONFUSION

The defenders are not quite ready for battle in the first round – the Ironjawz have just left a column of march, and the defenders were not expecting the orruks to attack so suddenly. Roll a dice before moving a defending unit on the first turn. On a roll of 1 or 2 the unit cannot move in that movement phase.

OVERRUN

The Ironjawz are eager to smash through the enemy line and move on. To represent this, Ironjawz units can make a bonus move after they attack in the combat phase, but only if there are no enemy models left within 3" of the Ironjawz unit. The bonus move is made in the same manner as a move in the movement phase, except that the unit cannot run.

VICTORY

Do not use any of the victory conditions on the *Warhammer Age of Sigmar* rules sheet. Instead, the Ironjawz immediately win a **major victory** if at least a quarter of the models that they deployed on the battlefield at the start of the battle are in the objective area shown on the deployment map. The Ironjawz player can instead claim a **minor victory** at any time that their general is in the objective area. Note that claiming a **minor victory** is optional – the Ironjawz player can refrain from doing so to have a chance of winning gloriously!

The defender wins a **major victory** if the Ironjawz fail to claim a victory before the end of the fifth turn.

HINTS & TIPS

This battle will be usually decided on whether the Ironjawz can smash through the centre of the defenders' line before the defending units from the two flanks can move to block their advance. You will find the battle is more enjoyable if the general of the Ironjawz army is not able to fly, or if they can, refrains from doing so in order to bypass the defending army and claim a **minor victory** by reaching the objective area. Winning in such a shallow way would be a hollow, inglorious thing, and because of that, we are sure no Ironjaw warlord worthy of the name would even consider doing such a thing!

THE GROWLING GATES

The Stormcast Eternals had raised the stronghold of Celestrium in shining Hysh, and from this city they sought to expand the domain of Sigmar. Connecting Celestrium to Ghur were the Growling Gates, and it was these portals that were the focus of their assault on the Chaos-held Beastfens.

The Growling Gates sprawled across the Beastfens. Six interconnected portals, they spread out around a central stronghold known as the Gorelight Gatefort, whose tallest spire shimmered with an ancient Realmgate. It was this central gate that connected all six portals to the fortress, but whose original destination lay in Hysh. For an age, Chaos tyrants had used the web of Realmgates to rule the surrounding lands with an iron fist. These were the enemies Pergus Brightshield and his Stormcast Eternals expected to face as they rode the lightning down toward the Growling Gates, his Strike Chamber attacking each of the portals at once. Little did the Stormcasts know, they were about to spring a trap.

Gordrakk had been pleased to see the first storm clouds gathering over the Growling Gates. His Weirdnobs had been right about where the lightning warriors would strike. Heeding Gordrakk's call, his Megafist had led tens of thousands of Ironjawz against the gates, stomping the Chaos defenders into the dust. The last of the Chaos forces had been finished off by his warclan, the Fang-krushas, and both the Gorelight Gatefort and the outlying portals now belonged to the Ironjawz. Gordrakk had faced Sigmar's Stormcast Eternals before and knew just how tough they could be, and so he had prepared some surprises for them.

Pergus' warriors stepped from the lightning onto the Gorelight Gatefort itself, his Judicators and Liberators spreading out and reacting quickly to the Chaos defenders lining the battlements. Bolts sang out, hammers crashed into steel and bodies tumbled to the ground as Pergus led his warriors in a charge toward the foe. For a moment, he thought his enemy broken, only to discover the fortress' defenders were no more than corpses crudely propped up to appear alive.

With their formation dangerously spread out, the Hammers of Sigmar had only a moment to react as a deafening 'Waaagh!' assailed their eardrums, and out of the keep charged a huge mob of Ironjawz. Just before the orruks

hit, the Liberators nearest to Pergus clanged together into a shield wall, but dozens more vanished under the green stampede. Iron slammed against sigmarite, and choppas rained down on golden helms as hammers thudded into green flesh. In moments, the Lord-Celestant and his men were enveloped by the Fang-krushas, reduced to a small golden island in a roiling sea of green.

Around the Growling Gates, the rest of the Stormcast Eternals fared no better than their lord. Some were caught by surprise as Ironjawz ran directly into the midst of the falling lightning bolts to attack, while others were assailed by Weirdnob Shamans, drunk on glowing green energy, who vomited death over the invaders. Under the crackling torrent some were blown to bits and others turned to vapour, while some lightning bolts were even turned back into the sky, disgorging their warriors hundreds of feet above the battlefield. For all the tricks, traps and sheer brutality of the Ironjawz, however, the Stormcasts fought back like true heroes of Azyr, not willing to give an inch before the ambushing greenskins.

Perched on a broken rampart of the Gorelight Gatefort's outer defences. Gordrakk watched and waited. This battle had only just begun, and duffing up the Stormcast Eternals was only part of his grand plan.

EYRIE OF
ECHOES

CLAWSTONE
DEEPWAY

HORNWILLOW
ARCH

GORELIGHT
GATEFORT

THIRSTING WASTE

WYRDWILD RIVER

DESOLATION'S
DOOR

DESERT OF THE LOST

MIRRORED
PATH

GLEAMGLOOM
PASSAGE

BLOODHAUNT WOODS

Across the Beastfens battle raged. While Lord-Celestant Pergus tried to wrest control of the Gorelight Gatefort from the Fang-krushas, the Stormcast Eternals at the outer gates fought furiously against greenskins from dozens of other warclans to link up with their brethren. A squad of Prosecutors swooped through the island portal of Hornwillow Arch to emerge from the mountainous Clawstone Deepway. The winged warriors arrived just in time to save the last Liberators gathered around the gate, breaking up a charging Brutefist with a rain of crackling hammers. Decimators that had cleared out the orruks infesting the Eyrie of Echoes broke free into the battles around Desolation's Door, driving back Ardfists with iron-cleaving blows. Lord-Relictor Dedrac himself fought to reclaim the Gleamgloom Passage, calling down arcing bolts from the storm to blast apart mobs of Ironjawz as a handful of Liberators fought valiantly at his side.

The successes of the Stormcasts, however, were but grazing blows upon the hide of a great beast. The warclans under Gordrakk numbered in the dozens, the Fang-krushas, Ironsunz and Zogboy's Choppas among the greenskins rampaging against the invaders. Brutefists forced shrinking knots of Stormcasts against the magical gateways, smashing them down into the piles of Chaos dead that still littered the ground. As they fell, Sigmar's warriors flashed back into the sky, much to the chagrin of the orruks who weren't done pounding them. On the cliffs before the Mirrored Path, Ironjawz grappled with the invaders. The burly orruks hurled Stormcasts off the edge, and just as often were borne with them to their deaths. In the confines of the Bloodhaunt Woods, Gorefists trampled everything in sight, as gruntas snorted and bit. Over it all was the thundering beat of the Warchanters, which shook even the huge Gorelight Gatefort to its skull-lined foundations.

Outside the walls of the Chaos bastion, Dakkbad Grotkicker and his Ironsunz waited for their chance to get stuck in. Some of the Ironjawz were already trying to barge their way through the warriors in front. A look from Gordrakk stopped the Megaboss in his tracks. Gordrakk was keeping the bulk of his force, and his best boys, back from the Gorelight Gatefort. A rumble of suppressed rage passed through the mass of Ironjawz, but none were foolish enough to cross the Fist of Gork.

Atop the massive Chaos keep, Pergus had cleared the ground around the central Realmgate, connecting him to his chamber and allowing a bloodied but defiant Dedrac to emerge via the Gleamgloom Passage with a dozen Liberators. With the arrival of the Lord-Relictor, the arcane mechanisms on the gate could be realigned to open the way to Hysh, and reinforcements from Celestrium could finally be called to turn the tide.

LORD-CELESTANT PERGUS BRIGHTSHIELD

In the opening engagements of the Realmgate Wars, Lord-Celestant Brightshield's Strike Chamber enjoyed great victories in Aqshy and Chamon, breaking open the Bloodbrass Gates, cleansing the slave pits of Yar Deep, and casting down the Balefeyr Lighthouse that stood above the Goresoul shores. Recently, however, things have changed. Unpredictable and savage, the Ironjawz have confounded the Hammers of Sigmar in numerous engagements, striking where they are least expected. Thrice now has Brightshield faced the Ironjawz, and each time it has been a costly encounter. To make matters worse, the belligerent orruks now seek the Stormcasts out, as they have earned a reputation as worthy opponents. Brightshield has learnt much in his battles with the Ironjawz, and his Strike Chamber is now embarking on a long war across the Carcass Kingdoms of Ghur against the Ironjaw warclans. The Lord-Celestant warns his brothers that a great enemy is rising in the beastlands, one that may well eclipse the Dark Gods' dominion.

One by one, the Growling Gates were retaken by the Ironjawz, bellowing lines of Brutes downing the few Stormcasts that remained in a tide of choppas and fists. Soon all that was left of the Strike Chamber was the thin cordon Pergus had created around the gate to Hysh. The Lord-Celestant knew their only hope of reinforcement was to realign the gate and call forth fresh warriors from Celestrium. He gave the signal, and over the hammering clash of arms and bestial screams of the Ironjawz, Lord-Relictor Dedrac began the incantations to manipulate the gate's wards. Spells woven at the beginning of the Age of Chaos began to unwind, and with a whisper of movement, invisible cogs spun to life. Gordrakk grinned as the gate began to shudder – then roared in anger as Dakkbad, tired of waiting, finally let loose his Ironsunz.

Where a moment before there had been only a steady, but stymied, flow of orruks, a flood of greenskins was unleashed. Atop his Maw-krusha Skullzcrakka, Dakkbad punched a hole in the Liberator lines, his boss choppa scorched by lightning as Stormcasts fell under its blade. At his back, Brutes, Gore-gruntas and Ardboys poured into the courtyard around the Realmgate, while Weirdnobs, shaking with the power of the Waaagh!, loosed green bolts into the fray. All the while, the drumming of the Warchanters carried over the battle, firing up the Ironjawz with its relentless tempo. With a look, Pergus and Dedrac shared the same thought: the orruks could not be allowed a path into Celestrium. Though he knew it would mean his death, Dedrac cut his chant short, and the magical seals crackled back into place.

Gordrakk bellowed loud enough to be heard from one end of the battle to the other. Incensed that Dakkbad had ruined his plans, he swooped toward the battle on his Maw-krusha, Bigteef. He considered giving the Megaboss a good kicking – but that could wait. As Gordrakk crashed down among the Stormcasts, Dedrac raised his staff to summon lightning and strike him down, but the orruk's axe, Kunnin', cut right through it, taking off the Lord-Relictor's head. Pergus leapt forward, his own blade catching a blow from Gordrakk's axe a second before it would have gutted him. But it only prolonged his life by seconds. With his back against the gate, Pergus was driven to the ground under the Maw-krusha's fists. A moment before Gordrakk's twin axes fell upon his skull, Pergus vowed vengeance with his last breath.

Although the Ironjawz may appear to be the epitome of simple-minded brutality and aggression, there are times when they can be surprisingly cunning. Admittedly, this doesn't happen all that often, but every now and then an Ironjaw Megaboss will take it into their head that it would be a right good laugh to trick an opponent before they duff them over.

Some especially intelligent Ironjaw warlords will even go as far as to use a cunning battle plan when the situation warrants it, rather than on a whim – for example, when they are heavily outnumbered or need to capture a well-protected objective. Gordrakk's ambush at the Growling Gates is an example of just such a battle, but many others can be found in the bloody histories of the Mortal Realms.

THE ARMIES

One player commands an Ironjawz army, and the other commands the marks that the Ironjawz are hoping to dupe.

IRONJAWZ' OBJECTIVES

Your boss has ordered you to capture a vital objective. Unfortunately it is heavily protected by the enemy, and you are not sure that the kind of head-on assault you usually prefer will work. Because of this, you have decided to be dead cunning, and so have ordered your boys to sneak up on the enemy and attack them suddenly from all sides. You've even held back a small reserve, which you can use to reinforce your lads wherever you think help is needed. You are certain that this sneaky plan will ensure you can both capture the objective and duff over the enemy army – it is a scheme worthy of Mork himself!

THE MARK'S OBJECTIVES

You have been ordered to defend a vital objective from an Ironjaw attack. You had expected the orruks to attack you head-on as they have always done in the past, but for some reason the expected assault has not taken place. In fact, things have been unnaturally quiet, and you are now worried that the Ironjawz are up to something. In the circumstances, you have little choice but to deploy your army to cover all of the approaches to the objective, and then be ready to respond to whatever sort of attack the orruks decide to throw at you. As long as you react quickly enough, you are sure you can protect the objective from any orruk attack.

HEY, SUCKER!

Before the battle starts, the players take part in a dice game to determine how effectively the mark was tricked by the Ironjawz' sneaky plan. All that is needed to play the game is a six-sided dice.

The mark must first look away. The Ironjawz player then places the dice on the table with a number of their choice face-up, and then hides it with their hand so the mark cannot see which number was chosen. The Ironjawz player then says 'Hey, Sucker!' out loud. The mark can now look back, and must say 'Odd' or 'Even' – the dice is then revealed. If the mark's guess was right, they win, and if the mark's guess was wrong, the Ironjawz player wins. The game is played a total of three times, and the Ironjawz player is allowed to pick one Cunnin' Trick from those listed on the following pages for each time they win.

THE BATTLEFIELD

The battle takes place on a plain, at the centre of which stands the objective of the Ironjawz' attack. Around the plain are four regions from which the Ironjawz can attack. The objective must be represented by a scenery model – we recommend using a Baleful Realmgate, Dragonfate Dais or Numinous Occulum. Place the objective at the centre of the battlefield, and then generate additional scenery for the battle as described on the *Warhammer Age of Sigmar* rules sheet.

SET-UP

The mark sets up first, anywhere in the central area of the battlefield, as shown on the deployment map.

The Ironjawz set up second in the four outer regions, more than 6" from any enemy units. No more than a quarter of the units from the Ironjawz army can be set up in each area. In addition, up to a quarter of the units in the Ironjawz army can be set up in reserve, entering the battle later as reinforcements (see the next page).

FIRST TURN

The Ironjawz take the first turn in the first battle round.

CUNNIN' TRICKS

As noted on the previous page, the Ironjawz player is allowed to pick up to three Cunnin' Tricks to use during the battle, depending on how well they did in the 'Hey, Sucker!' dice game.

WEIRDNOB APOCALYPSE

All the wizards in the Ironjawz army have been filled to the brim with magical energy before the battle starts.

Because of this, each wizard can attempt to cast up to three spells in the first Ironjawz hero phase, instead of the number of spells they are normally allowed to cast.

UNLEASH THE FLOODGATES

The Ironjawz surge towards the enemy at the start of the battle. Roll three dice rather than two when determining charge moves in the first Ironjawz charge phase. In addition, units in the Ironjawz army can attempt to charge if they are within 18" of the enemy, rather than only 12".

ON THE RAMPAGE

The Ironjawz unleash a frenzy of destruction at the start of the battle. There are two combat phases, one after the other, in the first Ironjawz turn. Complete all of the attacks in the first combat phase before starting the

second one. Note that this means that the mark will get to fight twice during the Ironjawz turn as well!

SURPRISE ATTACK

The enemy are completely unprepared for the attack. Subtract 1 from the hit rolls of all attacks made by any of the mark's units in the first battle round.

REINFORCEMENTS

The Ironjawz player can set up a quarter of their army in reserve. The Ironjawz player must roll a dice for each reserve unit at the end of each Ironjawz movement phase, subtracting 2 from the roll if they failed to win any games of 'Hey, Sucker!'. On a roll of 2 or more, the Ironjawz player can set up the unit or keep it in reserve. On a roll of 1 or less, the unit must be deployed (they got impatient), and the mark can choose where it is set up!

Reserves can be set up in any of the Ironjawz' territories. All models in the reserve unit must be set up in the same area, more than 6" from the enemy, but different units can be set up in different areas.

VICTORY

The side that controls the objective at the end of the fourth turn wins a **major victory**. A side controls the objective if they have models within 3" of it and there are no enemy models within 3". If neither side controls the objective, the battle is a draw.

THE
GREEN
HORDES

WARSCROLLS

The warriors and creatures that battle in the Mortal Realms are incredibly diverse, each one fighting with their own unique weapons and combat abilities. To represent this, every model has a warscroll that lists the characteristics, weapons and abilities that apply to the model.

Every Citadel Miniature in the Warhammer range has its own warscroll, which provides you with all of the information needed to use that model in a game of *Warhammer Age of Sigmar*. This means that you can use any Citadel Miniatures in your collection as part of an army as long as you have the right warscrolls.

When fighting a battle, simply refer to the warscrolls for the models you are using. Warscrolls for all of the other models in the *Warhammer Age of Sigmar* range are available from Games Workshop. Just visit our website at games-workshop.com for more information on how to obtain them.

The key below explains what you will find on a warscroll, and the *Warhammer Age of Sigmar* rules sheet explains how this information is used in a game. The warscroll also includes a picture of a unit of the models that the warscroll describes, and a short piece of text explaining the background for the models and how they fight.

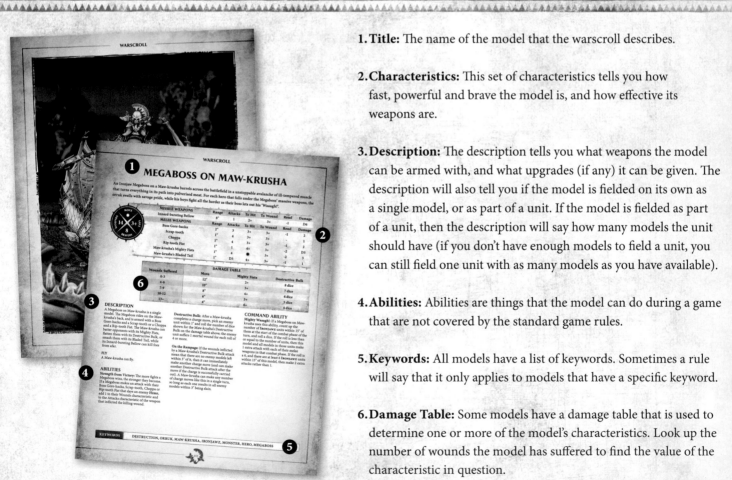

1. **Title:** The name of the model that the warscroll describes.

2. **Characteristics:** This set of characteristics tells you how fast, powerful and brave the model is, and how effective its weapons are.

3. **Description:** The description tells you what weapons the model can be armed with, and what upgrades (if any) it can be given. The description will also tell you if the model is fielded on its own as a single model, or as part of a unit. If the model is fielded as part of a unit, then the description will say how many models the unit should have (if you don't have enough models to field a unit, you can still field one unit with as many models as you have available).

4. **Abilities:** Abilities are things that the model can do during a game that are not covered by the standard game rules.

5. **Keywords:** All models have a list of keywords. Sometimes a rule will say that it only applies to models that have a specific keyword.

6. **Damage Table:** Some models have a damage table that is used to determine one or more of the model's characteristics. Look up the number of wounds the model has suffered to find the value of the characteristic in question.

HINTS & TIPS

Modifiers: Many warscrolls include modifiers that can affect characteristics. For example, a rule might add 1 to the Move characteristic of a model, or subtract 1 from the result of a hit roll. Modifiers are cumulative.

Random Values: Sometimes, the Move or weapon characteristics on a warscroll will have random values. For example, the Move characteristic for a model might be 2D6 (two dice rolls added together), whereas the Attacks characteristic of a weapon might be D6.

When a unit with a random Move characteristic is selected to move in the movement phase, roll the indicated number of dice. The total of the dice rolled is the Move characteristic for all models in the unit for the duration of that movement phase.

Generate any random values for a weapon (except Damage) each time it is chosen as the weapon for an attack.

Roll once and apply the result to all such weapons being used in the attack. The result applies for the rest of that phase. For Damage, generate a value for each weapon that inflicts damage.

When to Use Abilities: Abilities that are used at the start of a phase must be carried out before any other actions. By the same token, abilities used at the end of the phase are carried out after all normal activities for the phase are complete.

If you can use several abilities at the same time, you can decide in which order they are used. If both players can carry out abilities at the same time, the player whose turn is taking place uses their abilities first.

Save of '-': Some models have a Save of '-'. This means that they automatically fail all save rolls (do not make the roll, even if modifiers apply).

Keywords: Keywords are sometimes linked to (or tagged) by a rule. For example, a rule might say that it applies to 'all IRONJAWZ'. This means that it would apply to models that have the Ironjawz keyword on their warscroll.

Keywords can also be a useful way to decide which models to include in an army. For example, if you want to field an Ironjawz army, just use models that have the Ironjawz keyword.

Minimum Range: Some weapons have a minimum range. For example 6"-48". The weapon cannot shoot at an enemy unit that is within the minimum range.

Weapons: Some models can be armed with two identical weapons. When the model attacks with these weapons, do not double the number of attacks that the weapons make; usually, the model gets an additional ability instead.

GORDRAKK, THE FIST OF GORK

Gordrakk is the biggest and the baddest Ironjaw boss about, and he claims all greenskins for his Great Waaagh!. With his twin axes, Smasha and Kunnin', he lops off heads and cracks open skulls, while beneath his iron-shod boots, the Megaboss' huge Maw-krusha, Bigteef, crushes enemies to pulp, or bursts their innards with a deafening bellow.

MOVE ☀
WOUNDS 15
SAVE 3+
BRAVERY 8

MISSILE WEAPONS	Range	Attacks	To Hit	To Wound	Rend	Damage
Innard-bursting Bellow	8"	1	2+	3+	-1	D6
MELEE WEAPONS	Range	Attacks	To Hit	To Wound	Rend	Damage
Smasha	1"	5	2+	3+	-1	2
Kunnin'	1"	5	2+	3+	-	1
Bigteef's Mighty Fists	1"	5	☀	3+	-2	3
Bigteef's Bladed Tail	1"	3	4+	3+	-1	1

DAMAGE TABLE			
Wounds Suffered	Move	Mighty Fists	Destructive Bulk
0-3	12"	2+	8 dice
4-6	10"	3+	7 dice
7-9	8"	4+	6 dice
10-12	6"	5+	5 dice
13+	4"	6+	4 dice

DESCRIPTION

Gordrakk, the Fist of Gork, is a single model. Gordrakk is armed with two axes, one called Smasha and the other Kunnin'. He rides into battle on the back of a huge Maw-krusha called Bigteef, who batters opponents with his Mighty Fists, flattens them with his Destructive Bulk, and smashes them with his Bladed Tail. Even his Innard-bursting Bellow can kill foes!

FLY

Bigteef can fly.

ABILITIES

Smasha: Smasha is filled with the brutal power of Gork, making it especially lethal to enemy champions. Wound rolls of 6 or more inflict D3 mortal wounds if the target is a **Hero** instead of their normal damage.

Kunnin': Kunnin' is filled with the kunnin' power of Mork, and it seeks out enemy wizards to slay. Wound rolls of 4 or more inflict D3 mortal wounds if the target is a **Wizard** instead of their normal damage.

Strength from Victory: The more fights a Megaboss wins, the stronger they become. If Gordrakk makes an attack with Smasha or Kunnin' that slays an enemy **Hero**, add 1 to his Wounds characteristic and to the Attacks characteristic of the weapon that inflicted the killing wound.

Destructive Bulk: After Bigteef completes a charge move, pick an enemy unit within 1" and roll the number of dice shown for his Destructive Bulk on the damage table above; the enemy unit suffers 1 mortal wound for each roll of 4 or more.

On the Rampage: If the wounds inflicted by Bigteef's Destructive Bulk attack mean that there are no enemy models left within 3" of him, then he can immediately make another charge move (and can make another Destructive Bulk attack after the move if the charge is successfully carried out). Bigteef can make any number of charge moves like this in a single turn, so long as each one results in all enemy models within 3" being slain.

COMMAND ABILITY

Voice of Gork: Gordrakk's bellow carries the elemental force of his brutal god, and inspires his forces to surge into the enemy, hacking, bludgeoning and stomping with abandon. Once per battle, in your hero phase, you can pick a **Destruction** unit that is within 20" of Gordrakk. In the following charge phase, that unit can declare a charge if it is within 18" of the enemy, and you can roll three dice to determine the distance it can charge. In addition, the unit makes 2 extra attacks with each of its melee weapons in the following combat phase. If the unit you chose is part of a warscroll battalion, then these benefits also apply to all other units from the battalion.

MEGABOSS ON MAW-KRUSHA

An Ironjaw Megaboss on a Maw-krusha barrels across the battlefield in a unstoppable avalanche of ill-tempered muscle that turns everything in its path into pulverised meat. For each hero that falls under the Megaboss' massive weapons, the orruk swells with savage pride, while his boys fight all the harder as their boss lets out his 'Waaagh!'.

MOVE ✶
WOUNDS 14
SAVE 3+
BRAVERY 8

MISSILE WEAPONS	Range	Attacks	To Hit	To Wound	Rend	Damage
Innard-bursting Bellow	8"	1	2+	3+	-1	D6
MELEE WEAPONS	Range	Attacks	To Hit	To Wound	Rend	Damage
Boss Gore-hacka	2"	3	3+	3+	-1	2
Scrap-tooth	1"	4	3+	3+	-	1
Choppa	1"	4	3+	3+	-1	2
Rip-tooth Fist	1"	1	4+	3+	-2	D3
Maw-krusha's Mighty Fists	1"	4	✶	3+	-2	3
Maw-krusha's Bladed Tail	1"	D3	4+	3+	-1	1

DAMAGE TABLE			
Wounds Suffered	Move	Mighty Fists	Destructive Bulk
0-3	12"	2+	8 dice
4-6	10"	3+	7 dice
7-9	8"	4+	6 dice
10-12	6"	5+	5 dice
13+	4"	6+	4 dice

DESCRIPTION
A Megaboss on Maw-krusha is a single model. The Megaboss rides on the Maw-krusha's back, and is armed with a Boss Gore-hacka and a Scrap-tooth or a Choppa and a Rip-tooth Fist. The Maw-krusha can batter opponents with its Mighty Fists, flatten them with its Destructive Bulk, or smash them with its Bladed Tail, while its Innard-bursting Bellow can kill foes from afar.

FLY
A Maw-krusha can fly.

ABILITIES
Strength from Victory: The more fights a Megaboss wins, the stronger they become. If a Megaboss makes an attack with their Boss Gore-hacka, Scrap-tooth, Choppa or Rip-tooth Fist that slays an enemy **HERO**, add 1 to their Wounds characteristic and to the Attacks characteristic of the weapon that inflicted the killing wound.

Destructive Bulk: After a Maw-krusha completes a charge move, pick an enemy unit within 1" and roll the number of dice shown for the Maw-krusha's Destructive Bulk on the damage table above; the enemy unit suffers 1 mortal wound for each roll of 4 or more.

On the Rampage: If the wounds inflicted by a Maw-krusha's Destructive Bulk attack mean that there are no enemy models left within 3" of it, then it can immediately make another charge move (and can make another Destructive Bulk attack after the move if the charge is successfully carried out). A Maw-krusha can make any number of charge moves like this in a single turn, so long as each one results in all enemy models within 3" being slain.

COMMAND ABILITY
Mighty Waaagh!: If a Megaboss on Maw-krusha uses this ability, count up the number of **IRONJAWZ** units within 15" of them at the start of the combat phase of the turn, and roll a dice. If the roll is less than or equal to the number of units, then this model and all models in those units make 1 extra attack with each of their melee weapons in that combat phase. If the roll is a 6, and there are at least 6 **IRONJAWZ** units within 15" of this model, then make 2 extra attacks rather than 1.

ORRUK MEGABOSS

A Megaboss is the undisputed leader of his Ironjawz. Hordes of orruks follow the hulking warlord into the heart of battle where the best fighting is found. Clad in layers of iron and wielding massive weapons, Megabosses take great pleasure in besting enemy champions, while their barely contained Waaagh! energy drives their boys into a frenzy.

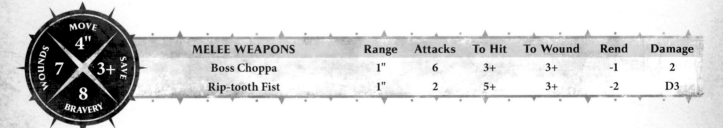

MOVE 4"
WOUNDS 7
SAVE 3+
BRAVERY 8

MELEE WEAPONS	Range	Attacks	To Hit	To Wound	Rend	Damage
Boss Choppa	1"	6	3+	3+	-1	2
Rip-tooth Fist	1"	2	5+	3+	-2	D3

DESCRIPTION
An Orruk Megaboss is a single model. They enter battle armed with a huge Boss Choppa in one hand, while their other hand is sheathed in a Rip-tooth Fist made of heavy iron.

ABILITIES
Go on Ladz, Get Stuck In!: An Orruk Megaboss can use a well-placed kick or thump to inspire the boys under their command to fight that little bit harder.

You can re-roll hit rolls of 1 for friendly units of **BRUTES** that are within 5" of this model when they make their attacks in the combat phase.

Strength from Victory: The more fights a Megaboss wins, the stronger they become. If a Megaboss makes an attack that slays an enemy **HERO**, add 1 to their Wounds characteristic and to the Attacks characteristic of their Boss Choppa.

COMMAND ABILITY
Waaagh!: If a Megaboss uses this ability, count up the number of **IRONJAWZ** units within 10" of them at the start of the combat phase of the turn, and roll a dice. If the roll is less than or equal to the number of units, then this model and all models in those units make 1 extra attack with their melee weapons in that combat phase. If the roll is 6 or more, and there are at least 6 **IRONJAWZ** units within 10" of this model, then make 2 extra attacks rather than 1.

KEYWORDS	DESTRUCTION, ORRUK, IRONJAWZ, HERO, MEGABOSS

ORRUK WARCHANTER

Warchanters hammer out the drumbeat of the Waaagh! with their stikks, the booming rhythm calling all orruks to war. Wild-eyed rabble-rousers, their concussive tempo increases as battle is joined, the Warchanter thumping anything within reach. The resultant surge of Waaagh! energy courses through the Ironjawz, driving them into a frenzy of violence.

MOVE 4"
WOUNDS 6
SAVE 4+
BRAVERY 7

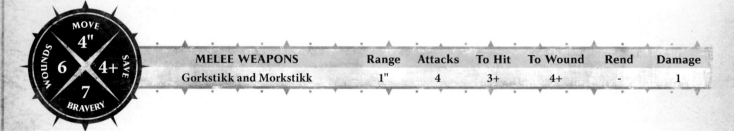

MELEE WEAPONS	Range	Attacks	To Hit	To Wound	Rend	Damage
Gorkstikk and Morkstikk	1"	4	3+	4+	-	1

DESCRIPTION
An Orruk Warchanter is a single model. They smash out rhythms on the skulls of their foes, hitting them with a Gorkstikk in one hand and a Morkstikk in the other.

ABILITIES
Warchanter's Beat: Each time you make a hit roll of 6 for a Warchanter's Gorkstikk and Morkstikk, you can make one additional attack with the weapon.

Frenzy of Violence: Pick one **IRONJAWZ** unit that is within 10" of the Warchanter in your hero phase. You can add 1 to all hit rolls made for that unit in the following combat phase.

KEYWORDS	DESTRUCTION, ORRUK, IRONJAWZ, HERO, TOTEM, WARCHANTER

ORRUK WEIRDNOB SHAMAN

Vomiting gouts of crackling green energy, Weirdnob Shamans stagger about the battlefield loosing the power of the Waaagh! upon the foes of the Ironjawz. Glowing green fists, rivers of lethal force and gargantuan stomping feet all assail the enemy as the shaman channels the savage impulses of hordes of bellowing, bashing orruks.

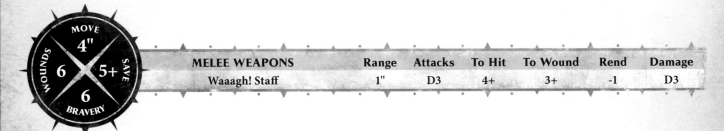

MOVE 4"
WOUNDS 6
SAVE 5+
BRAVERY 6

MELEE WEAPONS	Range	Attacks	To Hit	To Wound	Rend	Damage
Waaagh! Staff	1"	D3	4+	3+	-1	D3

DESCRIPTION

An Orruk Weirdnob Shaman is a single model. They are armed with a Waaagh! Staff.

ABILITIES

Power of the Waaagh!: Add 1 to a Weirdnob Shaman's casting or unbinding rolls if there are 10 or more **ORRUK** models within 10". Add 2 to the roll instead if there are 20 or more **ORRUK** models within 10". However, if the casting or unbinding roll was a double, then the closest **ORRUK** unit within 10" suffers D3 mortal wounds.

MAGIC

A Weirdnob Shaman is a wizard. They can attempt to cast one spell in each of your hero phases, and attempt to unbind one spell in each enemy hero phase. They know the Arcane Bolt, Mystic Shield, Green Puke and Foot of Gork spells.

Green Puke: Green Puke has a casting value of 8. Draw a straight line 2D6" long from the mouth of the Shaman. Each enemy unit crossed by the line suffers D3 mortal wounds.

Foot of Gork: Foot of Gork has a casting value of 10. If successfully cast, inflict D6 mortal wounds on a unit within 18". Then roll a dice – on a 4 or more Gork stomps again: resolve another D6 mortal wounds on an eligible unit. Gork keeps on stamping until you fail to roll a 4 or more.

KEYWORDS | DESTRUCTION, ORRUK, IRONJAWZ, HERO, WIZARD, WEIRDNOB SHAMAN

ORRUK BRUTES

Brutes lumber into battle seeking out the biggest monsters and the most violent enemies to batter into submission. Leading the way are their grinning bosses, savage warriors that like nothing more than to wrap their meaty fingers around their victim's neck and give them a good and proper bashing.

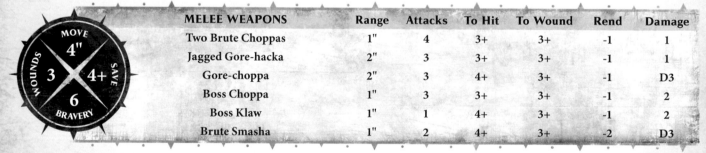

MELEE WEAPONS	Range	Attacks	To Hit	To Wound	Rend	Damage
Two Brute Choppas	1"	4	3+	3+	-1	1
Jagged Gore-hacka	2"	3	3+	3+	-1	1
Gore-choppa	2"	3	4+	3+	-1	D3
Boss Choppa	1"	3	3+	3+	-1	2
Boss Klaw	1"	1	4+	3+	-1	2
Brute Smasha	1"	2	4+	3+	-2	D3

MOVE 4"
WOUNDS 3
SAVE 4+
BRAVERY 6

DESCRIPTION
A unit of Orruk Brutes has five or more models. Some units of Orruk Brutes are armed with two Brute Choppas, while others prefer to use double-handed Jagged Gore-hackas. In either case, 1 in every 5 models may instead be armed with a massive Gore-choppa.

BRUTE BOSS
The leader of this unit is a Brute Boss, armed with a Boss Choppa or a Boss Klaw and a Brute Smasha.

ABILITIES
Duff Up da Big Thing: You can re-roll failed hit rolls for an Orruk Brute if the target has a Wounds characteristic of 4 or more.

Da Grab an' Bash: When you make attacks for a Brute Boss armed with a Boss Klaw and Brute Smasha, roll to hit with the Boss Klaw first. If it scores any hits, then a model from the target unit has been grabbed by the Klaw, and the Brute Smasha hits automatically as long as it is used to attack the same target unit.

KEYWORDS	DESTRUCTION, ORRUK, IRONJAWZ, BRUTES

ORRUK GORE-GRUNTAS

Gore-gruntas storm across the battlefield in a cacophony of hoofbeats and wild snorting. Gruntas rip up the ground and orruk riders bellow out war cries as the Gore-gruntas pull ahead of the Ironjaw charge. Leaving their foot-bound brothers behind, they are the first to crash with teeth-loosening force into the ranks of the opposing army.

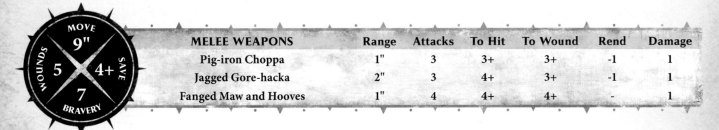

MOVE 9"
WOUNDS 5
SAVE 4+
BRAVERY 7

MELEE WEAPONS	Range	Attacks	To Hit	To Wound	Rend	Damage
Pig-iron Choppa	1"	3	3+	3+	-1	1
Jagged Gore-hacka	2"	3	4+	3+	-1	1
Fanged Maw and Hooves	1"	4	4+	4+	-	1

DESCRIPTION

A unit of Orruk Gore-gruntas has three or more models. The riders of some units of Gore-gruntas are armed with Pig-iron Choppas, while others carry Jagged Gore-hackas. Their mounts tear at the enemy with their Fanged Maws and Hooves.

GORE-GRUNTA BOSS

The leader of this unit is a Gore-grunta Boss. They make 4 attacks rather than 3.

ABILITIES

Gore-grunta Charge: Even by the destructive standards of the Ironjawz, a Gore-grunta charge is horrific to behold, enemy units vanishing under a roaring, grunting mass. However, a grunta needs a bit of a run-up to really get going! When you declare a charge with a unit of Gore-gruntas, measure the distance to the nearest enemy unit. If the distance is 8" or more and the charge is successful, the gruntas' Fanged Maw and Hooves attacks inflict D3 Damage rather than 1.

KEYWORDS DESTRUCTION, ORRUK, IRONJAWZ, GORE-GRUNTAS

ORRUK ARDBOYS

Tightly packed ranks of Ardboys plough into the fray to the sound of booming war drums and snapping banners. Shoulder plate to shoulder plate, the orruks fight ferociously, their violence focussed by the roaring orders of their boss and their eagerness to impress the mighty Ironjawz.

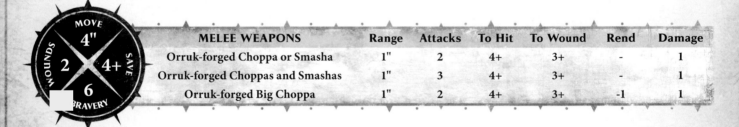

MOVE 4"
WOUNDS 2
SAVE 4+
BRAVERY 6

MELEE WEAPONS	Range	Attacks	To Hit	To Wound	Rend	Damage
Orruk-forged Choppa or Smasha	1"	2	4+	3+	-	1
Orruk-forged Choppas and Smashas	1"	3	4+	3+	-	1
Orruk-forged Big Choppa	1"	2	4+	3+	-1	1

DESCRIPTION

A unit of Ardboys has 10 or more models. Each unit is armed with an array of weapons; some of the boys carry Orruk-forged Choppas and Smashas, while others wield Orruk-forged Big Choppas. Some of the boys may instead carry a single Orruk-forged Choppa or Smasha and an Orruk-forged Shield.

ARDBOY BOSS

The leader of this unit is an Ardboy Boss. Add 1 to all of their hit rolls.

WAAAGH! DRUMMER

Models in this unit may be Waaagh! Drummers. Add 2 to charge rolls for a unit that includes any Waaagh! Drummers.

STANDARD BEARER

Models in this unit may be Standard Bearers. Standard Bearers can carry either an Orruk Banner or an Icon of Gork.

ABILITIES

Orruk Banner: You can add 2 to the Bravery of all models in a unit that includes any Orruk Banners, as long as the enemy are within 3" of the unit.

Icon of Gork: If a model flees from a unit that includes any of these Icons, roll a dice; on a 6 the Standard Bearer thumps the cowardly orruk – they return to the fight and don't flee.

Orruk-forged Shields: Roll a dice before allocating a wound to a model with an Orruk-forged Shield. On a roll of 6 the wound is ignored.

KEYWORDS DESTRUCTION, ORRUK, IRONJAWZ, ARDBOYS

WARSCROLL BATTALIONS

The warriors of the Mortal Realms often fight in battalions. Each of these deadly fighting formations consists of several units that are organised and trained to fight alongside each other. The units in warscroll battalions can employ special tactics on the battlefield, making them truly deadly foes.

If you wish, you can organise the units in your army into a warscroll battalion. Doing so will give you access to additional abilities that can be used by the units in the battalion. The information needed to use these powerful formations can be found on the warscroll battalion sheets that we publish for *Warhammer Age of Sigmar*. Each warscroll battalion sheet lists the units that make it up, and the rules for any additional abilities that units from the warscroll battalion can use.

When you are setting up, you can set up all of the units in a warscroll battalion instead of setting up a single unit. Alternatively, you can set up some of the units from a warscroll battalion, and set up any remaining units individually later on, or you can set up all of the units individually. For example, in a battle where each player takes it in turns to set up one unit, you could set up one, some or all of the units belonging to a warscroll battalion in your army.

On the following pages you will find a selection of warscroll battalions. Usually, a unit can only belong to one battalion, and so can only benefit from a single set of battalion abilities. However, some very large battalions include other, smaller battalions, and in this case it is possible for a unit to benefit from the abilities of two different battalions at the same time.

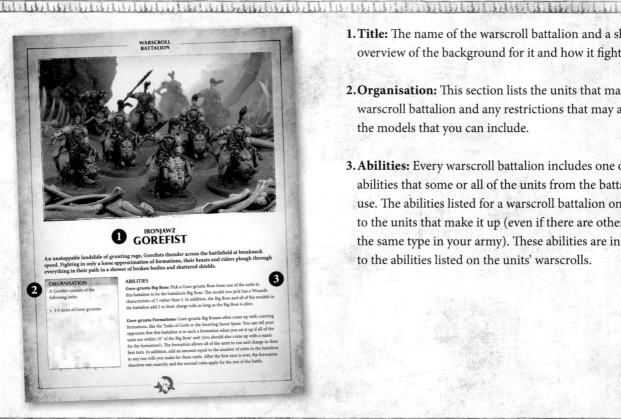

1. **Title:** The name of the warscroll battalion and a short overview of the background for it and how it fights.

2. **Organisation:** This section lists the units that make up the warscroll battalion and any restrictions that may apply to the models that you can include.

3. **Abilities:** Every warscroll battalion includes one or more abilities that some or all of the units from the battalion can use. The abilities listed for a warscroll battalion only apply to the units that make it up (even if there are other units of the same type in your army). These abilities are in addition to the abilities listed on the units' warscrolls.

IRONJAWZ
BRUTEFIST

The Brutefist lives up to its name with uncompromising force. A big boss takes pride in leading their fist in hammering through the thickest enemy ranks or heaviest defences like an armoured battering ram. There are few bastions safe from the fury of this blunt and brutal Ironjaw formation.

ORGANISATION

A Brutefist consists of the following units:

- 3-5 units of Orruk Brutes

ABILITIES

Brute Big Boss: Pick a Brute Boss from one of the units in this battalion to be the battalion's Big Boss. The model you pick has a Wounds characteristic of 5 rather than 3.

Green-skinned Battering Ram: A Brutefist is a living tide of destruction that can pulverise even the toughest of foes. In your hero phase, units from the battalion within 10" of its Brute Big Boss (including his own unit) can make a charge move as if it were the charge phase. If the charge is successful, pick one enemy unit within 3" of the unit that charged; it suffers D3 mortal wounds.

IRONJAWZ
GOREFIST

An unstoppable landslide of grunting rage, Gorefists thunder across the battlefield at breakneck speed. Fighting in only a loose approximation of formations, their beasts and riders plough through everything in their path in a shower of broken bodies and shattered shields.

ORGANISATION

A Gorefist consists of the following units:

- 3-5 units of Gore-gruntas

ABILITIES

Gore-grunta Big Boss: Pick a Gore-grunta Boss from one of the units in this battalion to be the battalion's Big Boss. The model you pick has a Wounds characteristic of 7 rather than 5.

Gore-grunta Formations: Gore-grunta Big Bosses often come up with cunning formations, like the Tusks of Gork or the Snorting Snout Spear. You can tell your opponent that this battalion is in such a formation when you set it up if all of the units are within 10" of the Big Boss' unit (you should also come up with a name for the formation!). The formation allows all of the units in the battalion to make a move of 15" in the hero phase of their first turn. The move is made as if it were the movement phase, except that the units cannot run. It does not stop the units from moving again normally later in the turn. After the first turn is over, the formation dissolves into anarchy and the normal rules apply for the rest of the battle.

IRONJAWZ
ARDFIST

Marching to the thumping beat of a Warchanter, the Ardboys gather, feeling the thunderous heartbeat of Gorkamorka reverberating in their chests. In seemingly endless numbers they come, eager to prove themselves the 'ardest greenskins around with booming war cries and brutal choppa blows.

ORGANISATION

An Ardfist consists of the following units:

- 1 Orruk Warchanter
- 3-5 units of Orruk Ardboys

ABILITIES

Drawn to the Waaagh!: The intoxicating beat drummed out by Orruk Warchanters draws many Ardboys out of the badlands. If the battalion's Warchanter is still alive in your hero phase, you can replace any units from the battalion that have been wiped out. The replacement unit is identical to the unit that was destroyed, and must be set up with all models within 6" of the edge of the battlefield, and more than 6" from any enemy units. Within these restrictions, it must be deployed as close to the battalion's Warchanter as possible. This counts as the unit's move for the following movement phase.

IRONJAWZ
WEIRDFIST

The savage power of the Waaagh! courses through a Weirdfist, cords of arcing green energy leaping from the massed greenskins and into the Weirdnob Shaman leading it. Jerking about even more alarmingly than normal, the Weirdnob unleashes this power in stunning displays of magical violence.

ORGANISATION

A Weirdfist consists of the following units:

- 1 Orruk Weirdnob Shaman
- 3-5 units chosen in any combination from the following list: Orruk Brutes, Orruk Gore-gruntas, Orruk Ardboys

ABILITIES

Weird Energy: The focussed energy absorbed by a Weirdnob Shaman in a Weirdfist overcharges their spells and incantations. In addition to the bonuses that the Weirdnob normally receives for being near other orruks, roll one dice for each unit from the battalion that is within 10" of the Weirdnob when an Arcane Bolt, Green Puke or Foot of Gork spell is successfully cast. Add 6" to the spell's range for each of these dice that rolls 1, 2 or 3, and add 1 to the mortal wounds inflicted by the spell for each roll of 4, 5 or 6. If the spell inflicts mortal wounds more than once, add the bonus each time!

IRONJAWZ
IRONFIST

Gathering up all the surrounding Ironjawz, a particularly aggressive boss bashes an Ironfist together to do some clobbering. While the boss keeps the boys in line, they charge ahead bawling out Waaagh! cries, needing little excuse to go and stomp on anyone foolish enough to try and stand in their way.

ORGANISATION

An Ironfist consists of the following units:

- 3-5 units chosen in any combination from the following list: Orruk Brutes, Orruk Gore-gruntas, Orruk Ardboys

ABILITIES

Ironfist Big Boss: Pick a Brute Boss or Gore-grunta Boss from the battalion to be its Big Boss, and add 2 to their Wounds characteristic.

'Ere We Go! 'Ere We Go! 'Ere We Go!: Urged on by their Big Boss, the mobs in this battalion are forever rushing forwards to get stuck into the fight. As long as the battalion's Big Boss has not been slain, in your hero phase each unit in this battalion can move D6". Roll separately for each unit, and then make its move in the same manner as a move in the movement phase, except that the unit cannot run.

IRONJAWZ
BRAWL

The ground shakes under the clanking, shuddering march of an Ironjaw Brawl. Filled with mobs of rowdy, bloody-minded orruks smashed together into mighty fists, it is a vast green tide that sweeps away armies, kingdoms and empires in an endless storm of violence.

ORGANISATION

A Brawl consists of the following units and warscroll battalions:

- 1 Orruk Megaboss or Orruk Megaboss on Maw-krusha
- 1 Orruk Warchanter
- 1 Orruk Weirdnob Shaman
- 5 battalions chosen in any combination from the following list: Brutefist, Gorefist, Ardfist, Weirdfist, Ironfist

COMMAND ABILITY

Big Waaagh!: The Megaboss that leads a Brawl is able to channel and direct the Waaagh! energy generated by their Warchanters and Weirdnob Shamans directly to their Big Bosses. To represent this, if the Megaboss of an Ironjaw Brawl is within 10" of a Warchanter and a Weirdnob Shaman from the battalion in the hero phase, then the Megaboss can use the Big Waaagh! command ability.

When a Megaboss calls a Big Waaagh!, all units from the Brawl that are within 15" of the Megaboss at the start of the following combat phase make 2 extra attacks with each of their melee weapons. Any units that don't receive this bonus but which are within 10" of a Big Boss from the Brawl make 1 extra attack instead with each of their melee weapons instead.

THE RULES

Warhammer Age of Sigmar puts you in command of a force of mighty warriors, monsters and war engines. This rules sheet contains everything you need to know in order to do battle amid strange and sorcerous realms, to unleash powerful magic, darken the skies with arrows, and crush your enemies in bloody combat!

THE ARMIES

Before the conflict begins, rival warlords gather their most powerful warriors.

In order to play, you must first muster your army from the miniatures in your collection. Armies can be as big as you like, and you can use as many models from your collection as you wish. The more units you decide to use, the longer the game will last and the more exciting it will be! Typically, a game with around a hundred miniatures per side will last for about an evening.

WARSCROLLS & UNITS

All models are described by warscrolls, which provide all of the rules for using them in the game. You will need warscrolls for the models you want to use.

Models fight in units. A unit can have one or more models, but cannot include models that use different warscrolls. A unit must be set up and finish any sort of move as a single group of models, with all models within 1" of at least one other model from their unit. If anything causes a unit to become split up during a battle, it must reform the next time that it moves.

TOOLS OF WAR

In order to fight a battle you will require a tape measure and some dice.

Distances in *Warhammer Age of Sigmar* are measured in inches ("), between the closest points of the models or units you're measuring to and from. You can measure distances whenever you wish. A model's base isn't considered part of the model – it's just there to help the model stand up – so don't include it when measuring distances.

Warhammer Age of Sigmar uses six-sided dice (sometimes abbreviated to D6). If a rule requires you to roll a D3, roll a dice and halve the total, rounding fractions up. Some rules allow you to re-roll a dice roll, which means you get to roll some or all of the dice again. You can never re-roll a dice more than once, and re-rolls happen before modifiers to the roll (if any) are applied.

THE BATTLEFIELD

Be they pillars of flame, altars of brass or haunted ruins, the realms are filled with strange sights and deadly obstacles.

Battles in *Warhammer Age of Sigmar* are fought across an infinite variety of exciting landscapes in the Mortal Realms, from desolate volcanic plains and treacherous sky temples, to lush jungles and cyclopean ruins. The dominion of Chaos is all-pervading, and no land is left untouched by the blight of war. These wildly fantastical landscapes are recreated whenever you play a game of *Warhammer Age of Sigmar*.

The table and scenery you use constitute your battlefield. A battlefield can be any flat surface upon which the models can stand for example a dining table or the floor – and can be any size or shape provided it's bigger than 3 feet square.

First you should decide in which of the seven Mortal Realms the battle will take place. For example, you might decide that your battle will take place in the Realm of Fire. Sometimes you'll need to know this in order to use certain abilities. If you can't agree on the realm, roll a dice, and whoever rolls highest decides.

The best battles are fought over lavishly designed and constructed landscapes, but whether you have a lot of scenery or only a small number of features doesn't matter! A good guide is at least 1 feature for every 2 foot square, but less is okay and more can make for a really interesting battle.

To help you decide the placement of your scenery, you can choose to roll two dice and add them together for each 2 foot square area of your battlefield and consult the following table:

Roll	Terrain Features
2-3	No terrain features.
4-5	2 terrain features.
6-8	1 terrain feature.
9-10	2 terrain features.
11-12	Choose from 0 to 3 terrain features.

MYSTERIOUS LANDSCAPES

The landscapes of the Mortal Realms can both aid and hinder your warriors. Unless stated otherwise, a model can be moved across scenery but not through it (so you can't move through a solid wall, or pass through a tree, but can choose to have a model climb up or over them). In addition, once you have set up all your scenery, either roll a dice on the following table or pick a rule from it for each terrain feature:

THE SCENERY TABLE

Roll	Scenery
1	**Damned:** If any of your units are within 3" of this terrain feature in your hero phase, you can declare that one is making a sacrifice. If you do so, the unit suffers D3 mortal wounds, but you can add 1 to all hit rolls for the unit until your next hero phase.
2	**Arcane:** Add 1 to the result of any casting or unbinding rolls made for a wizard within 3" of this terrain feature.
3	**Inspiring:** Add 1 to the Bravery of all units within 3" of this terrain feature.
4	**Deadly:** Roll a dice for any model that makes a run or charge move across, or finishing on, this terrain feature. On a roll of 1 the model is slain.
5	**Mystical:** Roll a dice in your hero phase for each of your units within 3" of this terrain feature. On a roll of 1 the unit is befuddled and can't be selected to cast spells, move or attack until your next hero phase. On a roll of 2-6 the unit is ensorcelled, and you can re-roll failed wound rolls for the unit until your next hero phase.
6	**Sinister:** Any of your units that are within 3" of this terrain feature in your hero phase cause fear until your next hero phase. Subtract 1 from the Bravery of any enemy units that are within 3" of one or more units that cause fear.

THE BATTLE BEGINS

Thunder rumbles high above as the armies take to the battlefield.

You are now ready for the battle to begin, but before it does you must set up your armies for the coming conflict.

SET-UP

Before setting up their armies, both players roll a dice, rolling again in the case of a tie. The player that rolls higher must divide the battlefield into two equal-sized halves; their opponent then picks one half to be their territory. Some examples of this are shown below.

Your Territory

Enemy Territory

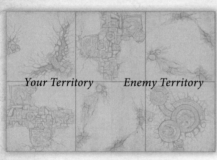

Your Territory   *Enemy Territory*

Your Territory

Enemy Territory

The players then alternate setting up units, one at a time, starting with the player that won the earlier dice roll. Models must be set up in their own territory, more than 12" from enemy territory.

You can continue setting up units until you have set up all the units you want to fight in this battle, or have run out of space. This is your army. Count the number of models in your army – this may come in useful later. Any remaining units are held in reserve, playing no part unless fate lends a hand.

The opposing player can continue to set up units. When they have finished, set-up is complete. The player that finishes setting up first always chooses who takes the first turn in the first battle round.

THE GENERAL

Once you have finished setting up all of your units, nominate one of the models you set up as your general. Your general has a command ability, as described in the rules for the hero phase on the next page.

GLORIOUS VICTORY

In the Mortal Realms battles are brutal and uncompromising – they are fought to the bitter end, with one side able to claim victory because it has destroyed its foe or there are no enemy models left on the field of battle. The victor can immediately claim a **major victory** and the honours and triumphs that are due to them, while the defeated must repair to their lair to lick their wounds and bear the shame of failure.

If it has not been possible to fight a battle to its conclusion or the outcome is not obvious, then a result of sorts can be calculated by comparing the number of models removed from play with the number of models originally set up for the battle for each army. Expressing these as percentages provides a simple way to determine the winner. Such a victory can only be claimed as a **minor victory**. For example, if one player lost 75% of their starting models, and the other player lost 50%, then the player that only lost 50% of their models could claim a minor victory.

Models added to your army during the game (for example, through summoning, reinforcements, reincarnation and so on) do not count towards the number of models in the army, but must be counted among the casualties an army suffers.

SUDDEN DEATH VICTORIES

Sometimes a player may attempt to achieve a sudden death victory. If one army has a third more models than the other, the outnumbered player can choose one objective from the sudden death table after generals are nominated. A **major victory** can be claimed immediately when the objective is achieved by the outnumbered player.

TRIUMPHS

After any sudden death objectives have been chosen, if your army won a major victory in its previous battle, roll a dice and look up the result on the triumph table to the right.

THE SUDDEN DEATH TABLE

Assassinate: The enemy player picks a unit with the **Hero**, **Wizard**, **Priest** or **Monster** keyword in their army. Slay the unit that they pick.

Blunt: The enemy player picks a unit with five or more models in their army. Slay the unit that they pick.

Endure: Have at least one model which started the battle on the battlefield still in play at the end of the sixth battle round.

Seize Ground: Pick one terrain feature in enemy territory. Have at least one friendly model within 3" of that feature at the end of the fourth battle round.

THE TRIUMPH TABLE

Roll	Triumph
1-2	**Blessed:** You can change the result of a single dice to the result of your choosing once during the battle.
3-4	**Inspired:** You can re-roll all of the failed hit rolls for one unit in your army in one combat phase.
5-6	**Empowered:** Add 1 to your general's Wounds characteristic.

BATTLE ROUNDS

Mighty armies crash together amid the spray of blood and the crackle of magic.

Warhammer Age of Sigmar is played in a series of battle rounds, each of which is split into two turns – one for each player. At the start of each battle round, both players roll a dice, rolling again in the case of a tie. The player that rolls highest decides who takes the first turn in that battle round. Each turn consists of the following phases:

1. Hero Phase
   Cast spells and use heroic abilities.
2. Movement Phase
   Move units across the battlefield.
3. Shooting Phase
   Attack with missile weapons.
4. Charge Phase
   Charge units into combat.
5. Combat Phase
   Pile in and attack with melee weapons.
6. Battleshock Phase
   Test the bravery of depleted units.

Once the first player has finished their turn, the second player takes theirs. Once the second player has also finished, the battle round is over and a new one begins.

PRE-BATTLE ABILITIES

Some warscrolls allow you to use an ability 'after set-up is complete'. These abilities are used before the first battle round. If both armies have abilities like this, both players roll a dice, re-rolling in the case of a tie. The player that rolls highest gets to use their abilities first, followed by their opponent.

HERO PHASE

As the armies close in, their leaders use sorcerous abilities, make sacrifices to the gods, or give strident commands.

In your hero phase you can use the wizards in your army to cast spells (see the rules for wizards on the last page of these rules).

In addition, other units in your army may have abilities on their warscrolls that can be used in the hero phase. Generally, these can only be used in your own hero phase. However, if an ability says it can be used in every hero phase, then it can be used in your opponent's hero phase as well as your own. If both players can use abilities in a hero phase, the player whose turn it is gets to use all of theirs first.

COMMAND ABILITY

In your hero phase, your general can use one command ability. All generals have the Inspiring Presence command ability, and some may have more on their warscroll.

Inspiring Presence: Pick a unit from your army that is within 12" of your general. The unit that you pick does not have to take battleshock tests until your next hero phase.

MOVEMENT PHASE

The ground shakes to the tread of marching feet as armies vie for position.

Start your movement phase by picking one of your units and moving each model in that unit until you've moved all the models you want to. You can then pick another unit to move, until you have moved as many of your units as you wish. No model can be moved more than once in each movement phase.

MOVING

A model can be moved in any direction, to a distance in inches equal to or less than the Move characteristic on its warscroll. It can be moved vertically in order to climb or cross scenery, but cannot be moved across other models. No part of the model may move further than the model's Move characteristic.

ENEMY MODELS

When you move a model in the movement phase, you may not move within 3" of any enemy models. Models from your army are friendly models, and models from the opposing army are enemy models.

Units starting the movement phase within 3" of an enemy unit can either remain stationary or retreat. If you choose to retreat, the unit must end its move more than 3" away from all enemy units. If a unit retreats, then it can't shoot or charge later that turn (see below).

RUNNING

When you pick a unit to move in the movement phase, you can declare that it will run. Roll a dice and add the result to the Move characteristic of all models in the unit for the movement phase. A unit that runs can't shoot or charge later that turn.

FLYING

If the warscroll for a model says that the model can fly, it can pass across models and scenery as if they were not there. It still may not finish the move within 3" of an enemy in the movement phase, and if it is already within 3" of an enemy it can only retreat or remain stationary.

SHOOTING PHASE

A storm of death breaks over the battle as arrows fall like rain and war machines hurl their deadly payloads.

In your shooting phase you can shoot with models armed with missile weapons.

Pick one of your units. You may not pick a unit that ran or retreated this turn. Each model in the unit attacks with all of the missile weapons it is armed with (see Attacking). After all of the models in the unit have shot, you can choose another unit to shoot with, until all units that can shoot have done so.

CHARGE PHASE

Howling bloodcurdling war cries, warriors hurl themselves into battle to slay with blade, hammer and claw.

Any of your units within 12" of the enemy in your charge phase can make a charge move. Pick an eligible unit and roll two dice. Each model in the unit can move this number in inches. You may not pick a unit that ran or retreated this turn, nor one that is within 3" of the enemy.

The first model you move must finish within ½" of an enemy model. If that's impossible, the charge has failed and no models in the charging unit can move in this phase. Once you've moved all the models in the unit, you can pick another eligible unit to make a charge, until all units that can charge have done so.

COMBAT PHASE

Carnage engulfs the battlefield as the warring armies tear each other apart.

Any unit that has charged or has models within 3" of an enemy unit can attack with its melee weapons in the combat phase.

The player whose turn it is picks a unit to attack with, then the opposing player must attack with a unit, and so on until all eligible units on both sides have attacked once each. If one side completes all its attacks first, then the other side completes all of its remaining attacks, one unit after another. No unit can be selected to attack more than once in each combat phase. An attack is split into two steps: first the unit piles in, and then you make attacks with the models in the unit.

Step 1: When you pile in, you may move each model in the unit up to 3" towards the closest enemy model. This will allow the models in the unit to get closer to the enemy in order to attack them.

Step 2: Each model in the unit attacks with all of the melee weapons it is armed with (see Attacking).

BATTLESHOCK PHASE

Even the bravest heart may quail when the horrors of battle take their toll.

In the battleshock phase, both players must take battleshock tests for units from their army that have had models slain during the turn. The player whose turn it is tests first.

To make a battleshock test, roll a dice and add the number of models from the unit that have been slain this turn. For each point by which the total exceeds the highest Bravery characteristic in the unit, one model in that unit must flee and is removed from play. Add 1 to the Bravery characteristic being used for every 10 models that are in the unit when the test is taken.

You must choose which models flee from the units you command.

ATTACKING

Blows hammer down upon the foe, inflicting bloody wounds.

When a unit attacks, you must first pick the target units for the attacks that the models in the unit will make, then make all of the attacks, and finally inflict any resulting damage on the target units.

The number of attacks a model can make is determined by the weapons that it is armed with. The weapon options a model has are listed in its description on its warscroll. Missile weapons can be used in the shooting phase, and melee weapons can be used in the combat phase. The number of attacks a model can make is equal to the Attacks characteristic for the weapons it can use.

PICKING TARGETS

First, you must pick the target units for the attacks. In order to attack an enemy unit, an enemy model from that unit must be in range of the attacking weapon (i.e. within the maximum distance, in inches, of the Range listed for the weapon making the attack), and visible to the attacker (if unsure, stoop down and get a look from behind the attacking model to see if the target is visible). For the purposes of determining visibility, an attacking model can see through other models in its unit.

If a model has more than one attack, you can split them between potential target units as you wish. If a model splits its attacks between two or more enemy units, resolve all of the attacks against one unit before moving onto the next one.

MAKING ATTACKS

Attacks can be made one at a time, or, in some cases, you can roll the dice for attacks together. The following attack sequence is used to make attacks one at a time:

1. Hit Roll: Roll a dice. If the roll equals or beats the attacking weapon's To Hit characteristic, then it scores a hit and you must make a wound roll. If not, the attack fails and the attack sequence ends.

2. Wound Roll: Roll a dice. If the roll equals or beats the attacking weapon's To Wound characteristic, then it causes damage and the opposing player must make a save roll. If not, the attack fails and the attack sequence ends.

3. Save Roll: The opposing player rolls a dice, modifying the roll by the attacking weapon's Rend characteristic. For example,

if a weapon has a -1 Rend characteristic, then 1 is subtracted from the save roll. If the result equals or beats the Save characteristic of the models in the target unit, the wound is saved and the attack sequence ends. If not, the attack is successful, and you must determine damage on the target unit.

4. Determine Damage: Once all of the attacks made by a unit have been carried out, each successful attack inflicts a number of wounds equal to the Damage characteristic of the weapon. Most weapons have a Damage characteristic of 1, but some can inflict 2 or more wounds, allowing them to cause grievous injuries to even the mightiest foe, or to cleave through more than one opponent with but a single blow!

In order to make several attacks at once, all of the attacks must have the same To Hit, To Wound, Rend and Damage characteristics, and must be directed at the same enemy unit. If this is the case, make all of the hit rolls at the same time, then all of the wound rolls, and finally all of the save rolls; then add up the total number of wounds caused.

INFLICTING DAMAGE

After all of the attacks made by a unit have been carried out, the player commanding the target unit allocates any wounds that are inflicted to models from the unit as they see fit (the models do not have to be within range or visible to an attacking unit). When inflicting damage, if you allocate a wound to a model, you must keep on allocating wounds to that model until either it is slain, or no more wounds remain to be allocated.

Once the number of wounds suffered by a model during the battle equals its Wounds characteristic, the model is slain. Place the slain model to one side – it is removed from play. Some warscrolls include abilities that allow wounds to be healed. A healed wound no longer has any effect. You can't heal wounds on a model that has been slain.

MORTAL WOUNDS

Some attacks inflict mortal wounds. Do not make hit, wound or save rolls for a mortal wound – just allocate the wounds to models from the target unit as described above.

COVER

If all models in a unit are within or on a terrain feature, you can add 1 to all save rolls for that unit to represent the cover they receive from the terrain. This modifier does not apply in the combat phase if the unit you are making saves for made a charge move in the same turn.

WIZARDS

The realms are saturated with magic, a seething source of power for those with the wit to wield it.

Some models are noted as being a wizard on their warscroll. You can use a wizard to cast spells in your hero phase, and can also use them to unbind spells in your opponent's hero phase. The number of spells a wizard can attempt to cast or unbind each turn is detailed on its warscroll.

CASTING SPELLS

All wizards can use the spells described below, as well as any spells listed on their warscroll. A wizard can only attempt to cast each spell once per turn.

To cast a spell, roll two dice. If the total is equal to or greater than the casting value of the spell, the spell is successfully cast.

If a spell is cast, the opposing player can choose any one of their wizards that is within 18" of the caster, and that can see them, and attempt to unbind the spell before its effects are applied. To unbind a spell, roll two dice. If the roll beats the roll used to cast the spell, then the spell's effects are negated. Only one attempt can be made to unbind a spell.

ARCANE BOLT

Arcane Bolt has a casting value of 5. If successfully cast, pick an enemy unit within 18" of the caster and which is visible to them. The unit you pick suffers D3 mortal wounds.

MYSTIC SHIELD

Mystic Shield has a casting value of 6. If successfully cast, pick the caster, or a friendly unit within 18" of the caster and which is visible to them. You can add 1 to all save rolls for the unit you pick until the start of your next hero phase.

THE MOST IMPORTANT RULE

In a game as detailed and wide-ranging as *Warhammer Age of Sigmar*, there may be times when you are not sure exactly how to resolve a situation that has come up during play. When this happens, have a quick chat with your opponent, and apply the solution that makes the most sense to you both (or seems the most fun!). If no single solution presents itself, both of you should roll a dice, and whoever rolls higher gets to choose what happens. Then you can get on with the fighting!